THE ARTISTS OF
TEREZIN

BY GERALD GREEN

FICTION:
Holocaust
Girl
An American Prophet
The Hostage Heart
Tourist
Blockbuster
Faking It
The Legion of Noble Christians
To Brooklyn with Love
The Heartless Light
The Lotus Eaters
The Last Angry Man
The Sword and the Sun

NONFICTION:
The Artists of Terezin
My Son the Jock
The Stones of Zion
The Portofino PTA
His Majesty O'Keefe (with Lawrence Klingman)

THE ARTISTS OF
TEREZIN

by

GERALD GREEN

HAWTHORN BOOKS, INC.
Publishers/New York
A Howard & Wyndham Company

We are grateful to Thomas and Vera Haas for permission to reproduce drawings from Bedrich Fritta's *Tomíčkovi* and to McGraw-Hill for permission to reprint a table of dates and eight poems from *I Never Saw a Butterfly*, edited by M. Volavkova (1964).

Jacket and Frontispiece illustration, *Seder* by Eva Meitner, age 11.

January 1979

THE ARTISTS OF TEREZIN

Text copyright © 1978, 1969 by Gerald Green. All photographs of illustrations within copyright © 1969 by Hawthorn Books, Inc, 260 Madison Avenue, New York, New York 10016. Copyright under International and Pan-American Copyright Conventions. All rights reserved, including the right to reproduce this book or portions thereof in any form, except for the inclusion of brief quotations in a review. All inquiries should be addressed to Hawthorn Books, Inc., 260 Madison Avenue, New York, New York 10016. This book was manufactured in the United States of America and published simultaneously in Canada by Prentice-hall of Canada, Limited, 1870 Birchmount Road, Scarborough, Ontario.

Library of Congress Catalog Card Number: 69–16020

ISBN: 0-8015-0420-1

2 3 4 5 6 7 8 9 10

To the Artists of Terezin

Preface

Many people who watched the television series "Holocaust" and read my novel of the same name have asked, was there in fact an incident concerning the artists of Terezin (Theresienstadt) in which a handful of courageous Jewish prisoners defied the SS and died so that a true artistic record of the horror might be saved for posterity.

The answer is yes.

The account in the TV drama and in the novel is somewhat fictionalized. But the basic elements are true—down to the interrogation conducted by Eichmann—and it grew out of this book, researched and written by me ten years ago.

It is appropriate that the story now be retold. Although the incident of the artists is perhaps only a footnote to the holocaust and pales before the satanic monstrousness of Auschwitz, it is a curiously arresting and revealing story.

For in Terezin, the "Paradeis ghetto," that false front built by the Nazis to deceive an all too believing outside world, men like Fritta, Ungar, Haas, and Fleischmann kept alive not only the glowing embers of creativity, but did not shy from making their art a weapon, a teaching device—pictures which terrify and engross the viewer, and in the end enlighten and elevate.

There is no fashionable ego in these pictures, no self-glorification, no "performing selves," no infatuation with one's own precious flesh. These men lived in hell under the constant threat of discovery, torture, and the ultimate transport east to the chambers and furnaces. They worked at their art secretly, and challenged the sadistic demons of the Reich daily. And miraculously their worked survived them.

There have been some who contend that the Terezin Jews who not only painted but staged operas and concerts and conducted language and philosophy classes, did the Nazis' work for them. I do not accept that for a minute. They tried, as best they knew, to keep human dignity and the intellect alive, to show their persecutors that even under appalling living conditions and the mutilation, torture, and annihilation they were functioning, sensitive, vibrant people.

None more brilliantly and heroically demonstrated this than the artists who are honored in this book and were depicted fictionally in the TV film and novel.

This is the true story. And it remains full of meaning, especially now that 120,000,000 Americans, through the power and pervasiveness of television, have been made keenly aware of the enormous crimes against Jews, indeed against humanity, committed in those years of shame.

GERALD GREEN

Stamford, Connecticut
May 1978

Contents

THE ARTISTS OF
TEREZIN

1

On July 25, 1945, in a small bleak hospital in Blankenhain, Germany, a displaced person named Otto Ungar died. Blankenhain is a tiny town south of Weimar, the city of Goethe, Schiller and the short-lived republic. Eight miles from Weimar is Buchenwald, a locale as firmly fixed in German history as Weimar.

In April, Otto Ungar had been liberated from Buchenwald. He was a Czech, a Jew, an artist, and a teacher. The cause of his death is uncertain—typhus, perhaps tuberculosis. Whatever the immediate cause, it was surely brought on by the tortures he had endured since 1942. That he had desperately clung to a shred of life for twelve weeks after his freedom is in itself remarkable. Emaciated, shrunken by disease, he had been a prisoner in Terezin, the main concentration camp in Czechoslovakia, and had spent over three months in the camp's dreadful *Kleine Festung*—the Little Fortress—an isolation prison for hard cases. Later he was sent to Auschwitz. And in January of 1945, he had been one of thousands of half-alive, moaning, stupefied wraiths who were sent across snowy Europe to Buchenwald in one of the worst of the death marches.

(A lunatic compulsion to move prisoners about from one horrible camp to another gripped the Germans as the war flickered to its end. Trains urgently needed for war matériel were suddenly commandeered to transport prisoners. A madman's game of musical chairs sent prisoners on endless death rides—Auschwitz to Buchenwald to Terezin to Lublin to Dachau —voyages without reason. It was as if by keeping up the pretense that the camps were a "going concern" of an efficient organization, of *Alles in Ordnung*, the Nazis hoped to soften the world's anger.)

Otto Ungar died, one obscure death added to the dreary statistics, the appalling actuarial tables bequeathed us by the Nazis. It was a commonplace death. Ungar—Czech, Jew, artist, teacher—was buried in Weimar. It is possible that he died consoled with the knowledge that his wife and daughter, who were in Terezin with him, and later suffered the tortures of its *Kleine Festung*, survived the holocaust.

The usual forms had to be completed on his death. Several patients in the small hospital had been in Buchenwald with the Czech, and they were able to contribute bits and pieces to the report. Yes, he was a Czech. How old? Oh, about forty-four. Born in Brno, educated in Prague. Taught at the Jewish secondary school in Brno—painting, mathematics, geometry. A shy fellow, a worrier. Not one of the tough ones. They'd seen him weeping. It was hard to believe he'd lived through so much— after what the SS had done to him.

He'd been singled out for special punishment. Something to do with some drawings, some paintings he'd done. That's why they'd stuck him in Terezin's *Kleine Festung*, the place for the prisoners who'd gotten into trouble. The SS guards had beaten him every day. Look what they'd done to his right hand.

The doctor and nurse attending Ungar had already noticed the hand. It had been crushed, mutilated, two fingers amputated. Scars, deformities were not unusual among concentration-camp survivors. In Ungar's case it seemed especially significant. An

2

artist, he'd offended the Germans somehow. He'd been made to pay for it.

To make the punishment fit the crime. Like Gilbert's "more humane Mikado," the Nazis prided themselves on their sense of appropriateness. But had Ungar learned his lesson? Evidently not. Some prisoners recalled his last days in Buchenwald. They had seen him crouched on his cold bed, hungry, silent, morose. In his maimed right hand he clutched a lump of coal. With pained, awkward movements, he tried to draw pictures on a scrap of paper. A stubborn man, Otto Ungar.

As far as I've been able to establish, these tortured Buchenwald sketches that Ungar drew with a piece of coal were never found. If they existed, one would be tempted to exhibit them in Buchenwald, captioned perhaps with Berenson's apothegm: *The purpose of art is to enhance life.*

Conceivably Ungar might object. His art, at least for the time he was a prisoner, did not noticeably enhance his life. Indeed— we shall see—it hastened his death. Yet there can be no argument that Ungar's works enrich and enlarge our lives. All of us who by the luck of the draw escaped the choking gas, the final bullet, the years of abomination are beneficiaries of Otto Ungar's mutilated right hand.

This book is about Otto Ungar, and Bedřich Fritta, and Leo Haas, and Karel Fleischmann, and the other artists of Terezin. Ungar died soon after his liberation. Fritta died as a result of beatings. Dr. Fleischmann and others were gassed. Leo Haas survived. They were the main actors in a revealing footnote to the Nazi era known to Czech graduates of Terezin as "the incident of the artists." I believe it is a footnote that tells us a great deal about the role of the artist, his obligations to his fellow man, and his response to wickedness. In the simplest of terms, these men died for daring to tell the truth through their art.

3

Incoming Transport (I) by Bedřich Fritta

Courtyard scene by Bedřich Fritta

They had not fought the Germans with guns or their bare hands —a response more difficult than some post-terror critics claim— but with their art. Was their response an effective one? It must have been. We shall observe the violent rage, the insensate fury to which mere sketches, water colors, lines on a sheet of paper, provoked the Germans.

We must start by stressing the compulsive efficiency the Germans lavished on the concentration camps and the Final Solution. There were systems on top of systems; categories; specialized designations; a madman's orderliness; a master plan for death. A crucial element in this system was their insistence that Terezin, or Theresienstadt, was really a country club, an old folks' home, a vacation spot for favored Jews. As we shall see, the Nazis succeeded in convincing many Europeans, including the International Red Cross, that the Jews were comfortable and

Courtyard in the Ghetto by Leo Haas

happy in Terezin. (I wonder if they had to work very hard at convincing most Europeans. It is stupefying to read how Europe kept giving the Germans the benefit of every doubt. Munich, polite references to "Herr Hitler," rationalizations of anti-Semitism, not to mention the enthusiastic cooperation of so many non-Germans—the eager Ukrainians of the exterminating teams, the Romanians who hung Jewish corpses in butcher shops, and the French gendarmes who rounded up the Jews of Paris in the infamous *grande rafle*.)

Terezin was a grand lie, a monstrous fraud. It was for exposing the sham that the artists were punished. A more apposite example of the proper function of art is difficult to imagine. All art, said Shaw, is didactic. Perhaps not *all* art. But much of it is. And there are times when it is the duty of art to be political.

Ungar, Fritta, Fleischmann, Haas, Bloch, Kien—artists of Terezin. Rather ordinary men, with some talent for painting, sketching, cartoon. Czech Jews, a mixed bag of *mittel-europäische* intellectuals, the sort of people who emerge from the mists of Central Europe as inevitable victims of the northern murderer. At times they seem to be the very people whom the Eichmanns and Heydrichs and Himmlers had in mind when they solemnly agreed to kill every Jew in Europe.

For example—Dr. Fleischmann. A dermatologist! Can anything sound more middle class, more in the tradition of the learned professional Jew? And a dermatologist who painted—and wrote poems! It is too facile to comment that while the Germans destroyed Dr. Fleischmann, his paintings live on. It is hardly a fair trade. I'm certain that, given his choice, the physician would have preferred having his life, and permitted his paintings to be burned. (Giacometti said that if there were a fire in his atelier, he would save the cat and let everything else go up in flames.)

7

No choice was given Dr. Fleischmann. He died; his paintings survived. They say he was a good-humored, outgoing, helpful man. The more I think of him with his scuffed bag (he practiced in Terezin), his water colors, his poems, the less I see him suited to play the role of martyr. There was nothing of the fanatic in Fleischmann, no odor of sanctity. (An odor of medical alcohol, perhaps.) Café sitter, concertgoer, good talker, family man, the kind of useful and intelligent Jew who was an affront and a rebuke to the Germans by his very existence. Of course he had to be killed.

I suspect the world grows weary of these deaths—single or mass. It is in the nature of things that Auschwitz should induce yawns. It was too monstrous to contemplate. Some years ago I wrote a novel on an aspect of the Nazi era—the stories of European Christians who had saved Jews. I was not wholly satisfied with it, and one reason, I discovered, was the inability of ordinary language to convey the appalling events. Dachau defeats syntax, grammar. It stuns reason, immobilizes the mind. There were moments when, seated in a darkened Paris apartment, reading through the sources, I would find myself sucking in my breath to see if I could imagine what it was like to be gassed. At night, reading about the children walking hand in hand into the chambers, I would wander into my own children's bedroom to make sure they were there—safe, secure American kids. And when I tried to weave my novel around these themes, I felt restricted, strait-jacketed.

Yet there is much still to be written about the holocaust. The themes are not exhausted. That is the real problem. It is not, as some critics contend, that the death camps have made topical writing impossible. Rather they have given us too *much* to write about. There are truths to be revealed, recesses examined, dark places illuminated. Buchenwald has shown many of us to be trivialists. I cannot accept the view that the concentra-

Incoming Transport (II) by Bedřich Fritta

tion camps have become irrelevant, even if the State Department assures me that Ho Chi Minh is worse than Hitler. The debts can never be paid; the full tapestry of those years will be forever unfinished; there will be gaps in the history books.

All these attitudes were reinforced in me when I began to talk to the handful of survivors of Terezin who live in the New York area. A few had known the artists personally. Some owned samples of their work. As I spoke with these graduates of hell, I encountered a luminous, admirable diversity, a will to live, and experience, and learn, that astounded me. I make no apologies for using a rather orotund phrase, but there is a *human spirit*. I cannot, for all my pessimism, accept the conclusion that Himmler was more typical of the human race than Dr. Fleischmann.

What was the basis of this vital quality in the Terezin survivors I met? I'm not certain. I don't claim it only for Jews, or even Czech Jews, or even Czech Jews who had lived through the camps. I am innocent enough to believe that there is a similar potential in each of us. We all carry a spiritual fingerprint. It is not necessarily honorable or beautiful or creative. Indeed, it can be horrid, destructive. Streicher and Bormann are too fresh in our memory. But with the greatest of hesitancy, I make bold to suggest that a good society will try to locate man's decent impulses, bring them to the surface, and encourage them gently and skillfully. Perhaps, in some dreadful manner, the compost of Nazi Europe had brought these qualities to fruition in the Terezin survivors to whom I spoke, and the artists of this book.

Whittaker Chambers once claimed he saw the devil. I think it was in a restaurant or a night club. I certainly believe him. (To establish my own *bona fides*, I've always believed the bulk of *his* testimony, not Alger Hiss'. Any man who could find implacable evil in the New Deal and conceive of himself as The

Artificial Limbs by Karel Fleischmann

Scenes of Terezin life by Karel Fleischmann

Teresín
A-II

Scene of Terezin life by Karel Fleischmann

Witness, on the order of De Lawd, must be believed.) But I have the feeling that some of my Terezin witnesses, Mrs. Ahlfeld-Schlesinger, Mr. and Mrs. Lebowitz, Fred Kantor, Norbert Troller, Mrs. Martha Klein von Peci, saw a good deal more of the devil, and knew him a lot better than Chambers. No matter how trying his ordeal, he was a reasonably well-fed, well-paid American magazine editor. I will match Otto Ungar's devil against the one Chambers saw, any day of the week. What I really suspect is that Chambers suffered from a dearth of real wickedness. He wrote mournfully of a world that would become "a stew of bones," but he was denied direct experience of Auschwitz.

A good imagination is a help in mystico-literary enterprises. Chambers had a well-developed one. So did other devil-observers, like Luther. And any number of Catholic saints. Yet I am obliged to regard the testimony of these witnesses, and all the holy persons in the Christian hagiography, as not being worth a tinker's damn compared to the devil who crushed Ungar's hand and beat Fritta into a bloody pulp. There is the weight of numbers on their side—six million supporting witnesses, none convinced of their holy rectitude, none anointed, none windy with the divine afflatus. And the majority of them were deceived to the end, convinced that it would never happen to them. Their devil was a great dissembler, a confidence man.

Disbelief in their doom runs like a muddy river through so much of this tragic time. The classic example was Herr Doktor Karl von Weinberg, deputy chairman of the consulting board of I. G. Farben, an elder statesmen of the great corporation. In 1933, Dr. Weinberg confidently told some visiting Du Pont officials that "although he was a Jew, he has given the [Nazi] movement his full stamp of approval." Evidently his approval was not wanted. At the age of eighty-one, Weinberg was shipped to Terezin, and confined to a special barracks for Jewish dignitaries —millionaires, nobility, former high-ranking officers, government ministers, all potential hostages. There, amid squalor and overcrowding, the I. G. Farben executive died after a gall-bladder operation. I met the woman who had nursed him during his illness, and in whose arms he died, Mrs. Martha Klein von Peci. She is a handsome gray-haired woman, spared because her late husband had been a distinguished Christian army officer in Austria. Mrs. Klein von Peci showed me a little book of remembrances she had kept in Terezin—poems, sketches, photos, clippings. There are good wishes from Baron and Baroness de-Hirsch, Jewish generals and colonels, industrialists, Rabbi Leo Baeck of Berlin, a roster of the élite.

There is a remarkable photograph of Herr Doktor Weinberg. A white-haired, small-featured man, decorations glitter in his lapel. His snowy breast is slashed with a wide satin ribbon. He is every millimeter the German tycoon. But I. G. Farben and Du Pont and his "full stamp of approval" did him little good. What could have Herr Doktor thought as he lay dying in the privileged barracks? That it was all a clerical oversight that someone at I. G. Farben would rectify after proper papers were expedited?

Weinberg was not alone in his refusal to believe the worst. Yet how can we blame them, particularly during the early years of the blight, when the Germans fed them lies, deceits, false promises? I submit it is much too easy today to argue that these powerless, alien people should have gone for the throats of the nearest SS men, seized the Luger and "taken one along."

Herr Doktor's attitude was surely extreme. I doubt that the little haberdasher or confectionery-store owner in Berlin whose windows were smashed on *Kristallnacht* was capable of giving the regime his "full stamp of approval." But there was resignation, acceptance, more than is comfortable to contemplate. Still . . . what were they to do? Take to the hills? Flee? In a Europe that had no use for them, a Europe conditioned by two thousand

In the Attic by Bedřich Fritta

years of sanctified hatred, taught to regard them as well-poison-
ers, deicides, agents of Satan, witches, child murderers?

So they were marched to the camps—their own officials
drawing up the lists, their own young men arranging the transports, their own people keeping records, assigning property. It
would all end, of course. It would have to. Evil would be de-
feated. God watches over us. Are we not His people? *Shema
Isroel Adonai Elohenu.*

How cunningly the Germans understood this! Their brutality and savagery are well known by now. But I think we do not
fully appreciate the sickening trickery they employed, all of it
heavy with a revolting outhouse humor. We read these accounts
of thirty years ago, and we hear again the booming, unashamed
laughter; we see those strange wide smirks. Truly they seem to
be smiling all the time.

Recall, if you will, those photographs from Berlin and
Munich of the early Nazi years—old Jews scrubbing the streets,
Jews playing horsey for SS hoodlums, Jewish families walking
nervously down a cobbled street. Always, always, in the background are these grinning louts, these bovine heaps of flesh,
these woodenheaded uniformed clods, these final flowerings of
dear old Europe! And they smile. What are they laughing about?
What is so funny about old Jews washing the streets, about
Jewish children with chalk marks on their backs?

There are times when I feel that the Terezin concept, the
careful development of this "model ghetto," this old folks'
home, was accompanied by a good deal of hearty German laughter! Lots of creamy Pilsen beer and Braunschweiger must have
been gobbled as they dreamed up Terezin—the *nice* concentration camp, the little village for the privileged and the old! Reject
forever the myth that Nordic people are solemn, work-driven,
unsmiling. Not true. Rarely does one encounter such bubbling
joy, such gaiety, as manifests itself in German planning vis-à-vis

Ravens by Bedřich Fritta

the Jews. How thoroughly they enjoyed their work! Explosive guffaws, flat smiles, blue eyes rolling and winking, fat thighs slapped. Imagine the laughter at Gross-Wannsee in January of 1942, when Heydrich decreed that Terezin would have "special" status—a camp for the aged, the ill, Jewish veterans, Jews married to Aryans, other special categories. It almost, in light of the appalling toll of dead it produced, seems to have been an interminable bloody joke.

This obscene humor becomes more apparent when one studies the various names the Nazis gave to Terezin. At different times it was known as *Theresienbad* (Spa Terezin), *Reichsaltersheim* (State Home for the Aged), *Judische Selbtsverwaltung* (Jewish Self-Administration), and in some of the early propaganda, *Paradeisghetto*. Like all involved lies, it had a germ of truth. The fact of the matter was that if you were young, strong, had a good job, or were a privileged person, Terezin was a vast improvement over Bergen-Belsen or Buchenwald. That is to say, it was better until you were shipped to Auschwitz and death.

For the bald truth is that after all its special functions are discounted, Terezin was a collection point for Auschwitz. It served to further the Final Solution, to assemble a lot of Jews in one place, so that they might be efficiently dispatched to the gas chambers.

It was a strange place in many ways. Early in its history, Jews, thanks to the corruption of the Gestapo, could "buy" their way into the camp. This entrapment was called "protective custody." A Jew desirous of going to the *Paradeisghetto* surrendered all his property to the Gestapo, assured that he would be reimbursed by the Jewish Council of Terezin. Once in the camp, he got back nothing, and had, in all likelihood, gone willingly to extermination.

This was the truth about the "model ghetto." But it served

the Nazis superbly. It was propagandized. Foreign dignitaries were paraded through Terezin to prove that the Jews were treated well. (We shall come in due course to the historic Red Cross inspection of 1944, which was closely connected with the death of the artists.) So convinced were the Germans with the credibility of Terezin, the pervasiveness of the fraud, that as late as April of 1945, Himmler was certain that reports of the death camps abroad had been discounted, that the world did not believe in Auschwitz or Dachau any more! Listen to the wheedling voice of the mass murderer, as he bargained for respectability, for his skin, with Dr. Norbert Masur of the World Jewish Congress:

Terezin is not a camp in the ordinary sense of the word, but a town inhabited by Jews and governed by them and in which every manner of work is to be done. This type of camp was designed by me and my friend Heydrich and so we intended all camps to be.

(But he does not refer to the 112,000 who died either in Terezin or after transport "east.")

Did the Nazis believe their own lies? Was Himmler sincere when he insisted that Terezin was "a town inhabited by Jews"? The temptation is sometimes strong to believe that they did. Yet why were they in such a frenzy to mop up the blood, to remove the scraps of brain and bone? A sense of guilt—or a fear of punishment? Had the mass murder of Jews been a mere tool to unite Europe behind them? Hitler kept insisting, with terrible accuracy, that most Europeans, notably Poles, Ukrainians, Croats, Latvians, Lithuanians, Romanians, Hungarians, and perhaps lesser numbers of Western Europeans, were in enthusiastic accord with his plans for the Jews. Perhaps the anti-Semitic campaign was only a lever, a prime gear, in his plan for world mastery.

Theater Performance in the Attic by Bedřich Fritta

Entertainment by Bedřich Fritta

Chimneys of the Bakeries in Terezin by Bedřich Fritta

Phantasy by Bedřich Fritta

I am afraid my own conclusion is quite the opposite. It is my conviction that what was paramount, mandatory and central to Hitler's program was murder. As I study the evidence, I am persuaded that the generative force of Nazism, the very core of their movement, was the killing of Jews. All other aspects of Nazism—employment, rearmament, world domination, Aryan supremacy—all these were secondary, and grew out of the compulsion to murder. They lusted for death. They were in covenant with Hell. They were greedy to inflict pain, torture, to maim and destroy children. This sustained them and motivated them. Everything else—conquest, industrial growth, aggrandizement—stemmed from the imperative to annihilate Jews.

What better witness than Hitler himself? In his underground bunker, ready to shove the revolver into his carious mouth, he found time to write a note explaining that it was all the Jews' fault, that he never wanted war, but that they, villains, shoved him into it. With Russian guns blasting his capital into rubble, he could dream only of murdering more Jews.

But I suspect a few Nazis harbored doubts. Had the Germans been convinced of their absolute right to murder Jews, had they all believed that they were fulfilling a European destiny two thousand years in the making, they should have bragged about Dachau! Buchenwald should have been proudly exhibited to the world, not as an object of shame, but as a national achievement, a Louvre, a Parthenon of German *Kultur*. "Would you believe it, M. Suisse," the SS guides should have told the visiting Red Cross delegation, "this oven can process ten thousand bodies a day, and with remarkably little ash! A firm in Dortmund designed the high-intensity burners. . . ."

I'm impelled to speculate that the Terezin fraud, this model ghetto, this old folks' home with its phony stores and fake coffee shop, its concerts and theater, was in part a product of this imperfectly understood suspicion on the part of some Nazis that they were nothing more than a gang of wicked bastards, for whom punishment was inevitable. The truly outrageous thing is that Terezin worked marvelously for them. It deceived its inmates. It prolonged the deception of many neutrals and many in the West. And although in this last function it may be said ultimately to have failed, it was utilized as an earnest of humanitarianism by Nazi leaders to the very end.

The lie of Terezin was so pervasive, so efficacious, that as late as the autumn and winter of 1944, it was enlisted to deceive both the Jews and the Red Cross in a giant hoax aimed at camouflaging the death camp par excellence, Auschwitz.

The scheme was essentially Nazi—cynical, complex, minutely planned. It began in September of 1944, when two transports of Jews totaling five thousand were sent from Terezin to Auschwitz. It should be pointed out that even at this late date many Jews refused to accept the ultimate horror. When the Terezin Jews arrived, old-timers at Auschwitz were stunned to see SS guards helping the aged from the crowded trains, carrying children, escorting the new arrivals to a special "family camp" where parents and youngsters could stay together—a rare privilege.

There was one other unusual privilege in this "family camp." The Jews were encouraged to write to friends and relatives at Terezin and to tell them how pleasant life was. Moreover, the very *name* Auschwitz was not to be used. Although they were but a few hundred meters from the gas chambers, they were told that they were occupying a new work camp, *Birkenau bei Neu-Berun!* Dutifully, they wrote of their good luck.

In December of 1944, another five thousand Terezin Jews came to Birkenau. They too were housed in the "family camp" and ordered to write letters postmarked "Birkenau." Soon Red

27

Courtyard scenes by Bedřich Fritta

Cross parcels arrived; life was hard but bearable.

In January of 1945, a delegation from Berlin that included SS Lieutenant Colonel Karl Adolf Eichmann, chief of the Gestapo's Jewish Section, and the head of the German Red Cross inspected the new work camp. Eichmann was especially interested in the school for Jewish children. He praised the cultural life. He had good words for everyone. The Red Cross was impressed.

On March 5, 1945, the SS commandant of Birkenau advised the Terezin Jews to prepare for transfer to a new camp called Heydebreck. At once, warnings from the Jewish underground trickled in: *There is no such place as Heydebreck; Heydebreck means the gas chambers.* But the SS, always prudent, had foreseen the possibility of revolt. Potential troublemakers were executed in isolation. Not until the Terezin Jews were in the underground rooms, where they were ordered to disrobe, did they fully understand the horrendous fraud; they all perished. Some battled the guards with bare hands and had to be driven to their death. They died singing *Hatikvah.*

And so the first shipment of Jews to Birkenau died. (There had been many prior shipments to death camps; this was the first one deliberately designed to mislead and deceive the remaining Jews at Terezin.) Before they were murdered, the Germans squeezed the last drop of value from their bodies. Two days before the gassings, they were given post cards to send to Terezin. They were dated March 25. The SS explained that "censorship would hold them up for a while."

Not every inmate of Terezin was deceived. A woman I met in New York, whom I shall call Mrs. Ruckmann, showed me one of these Birkenau cards dated March 25. It had been sent to her from her sister at Birkenau. Before leaving Terezin, Mrs. Ruckmann's sister had told her: "If my writing slants upward it will mean everything is all right. If it slants downward it means we are going to die."

The neat writing slants downward.

Soon a third Terezin group reached Birkenau. It was now evident that the "family camp" was one more swindle aimed at suppressing any rebellious notions at Terezin. Residents were systematically exterminated. But not before each doomed group wrote post cards of assurance to those still in Terezin.

There was a second function to the Terezin-Birkenau arrangement. The German Red Cross was getting edgy. Herr Niehaus, head of its foreign department, wrote nervously to Eichmann: "In view of the increasing inquiries from abroad about the different Jewish camps, it would seem that the repeatedly stated expediency of this planned visit to Birkenau is now even greater." But the International Red Cross, as it turned out, never bothered inspecting Birkenau. They were evidently so satisfied with earlier visits to Terezin that a tour of Birkenau was deemed superfluous. Herr Niehaus need not have been so concerned. Terezin had more than fulfilled its promise.

Is it worth reviewing the morbid statistics? I do so with a twinge of guilt. Once I heard Dorothy Thompson, in a radio debate many years ago, cry at Harry Golden, "There he goes with those six million dead again!" Yet the numbers are as good a threnody as any for this time:

Terezin served as a prison for about 76,000 Czech Jews from the so-called "Protektorat" of Bohemia and Moravia.

It also housed 42,000 Jews from Germany, 15,000 from Austria, 6,500 from various other countries.

That makes for a total of about 140,000 who passed through Terezin at one time or another. The average population at any one time is estimated to have been about 40,000—in a small town built for 7,000. Peak population was reached on September

18, 1942—58,491. The daily death rate set a record then also—156 dead every twenty-four hours.

There was no planned program of extermination at Terezin. It was a way station, a collection point. But 33,430 prisoners died there—of starvation, beatings, disease, exhaustion. *Almost one quarter of all who were interned!*

Roughly 87,000 prisoners were shipped from Terezin to other camps, including Auschwitz. Of this number, about 5 per cent survived. This means that about 78,000 died. If we add this to the 33,430 who perished in Terezin, we have approximately 112,000 who died in Terezin or after transport to the "East."

"While the Jews in Terezin are sitting in the café drinking coffee, eating cake, our soldiers have to bear all the burdens of a terrible war!" shouted Dr. Goebbels. I am not so sure he uttered these words with complete cynicism.

Terezin was a curio in the Nazi cabinet of horrors. The Germans seem to have been fascinated with it, particularly the varied, vigorous cultural life the Jews nurtured in the shadow of death. Who but Jews would bother staging *Carmen*, *The Bartered Bride*, or performing Verdi's *Requiem* on a diet of stale bread and thin soup, in a place where your first violinist or leading soprano might be at rehearsal one day—and in a filthy train bound for Auschwitz the next?

When the brilliant young Prague conductor Rafael Schächter led the *Requiem*, Eichmann himself attended the premiere, accompanied by his aide, SS Captain Moes, the man known to Jews as "the bird of death." One account of the incident describes Eichmann as reacting in a puzzled, lost manner, moved to a kind of reverie when his Jews sang *Dies Irae, Libera me, libera nos!* There is a good deal of the dilettante, the eager dabbler in the arts in many Germans. I think they reacted to the flourishing of art in Terezin with a dilettante's curiosity. They

Interior of the Terezin Temporary Synagogue by Otto Ungar

Portrait of an Old Woman by Otto Ungar

permitted the concerts, the lectures, the library, the art shows, and, it would seem, at times encouraged them.

But when art became an adversary, it had to be crushed. So long as performances and paintings were of a neutral, uncommitted nature, they were condoned. It was only when the artists of this book dared to paint the dreadful truth about Terezin, to use their talent as a weapon against brutality, that the fury of the jailers was aroused. Not for a moment do I mean to minimize the courage and dedication and talents of those who staged *Carmen*, lectured on Kant, distributed library books. All these activities preserved something noble and fine, and, we may be sure, preserved the sanity of thousands who passed through Terezin. But when the artist turned to his enemy and said, *You lie, and we will expose your lies; you are the enemies of decency and civilization, and we will show you to the world for what you really are*—only then did the artist have to be obliterated, only then was Ungar's right hand crushed, were Fritta and Felix Bloch beaten to death.

Study Otto Ungar's water color *The Coming of a Transport*, and you will understand why he was thrown into the *Kleine Festung* along with his wife and child, why he was beaten and tortured daily, and why the jack boots and bludgeon were used to destroy his hand. Ungar's people are not joyful vacationers; they are arriving at no old folks' home, they are under no illusions about what is in store for them. The very numbers depending from their necks speak of their doom. No one could see this painting and still believe that Terezin was a happy village.

The Coming of a Transport by Otto Ungar

View of the Ghetto by Bedřich Fritta

2

The town of Theresienstadt, or Terezin, to use its Czech name, was founded in 1780 by the Emperor Josef II in honor of his mother, the inescapable Maria Theresa. The old lady cannot be avoided in Central Europe. She is as much a part of the countryside as the meandering streams and the fat white geese. In such a setting, about thirty miles north of Prague, lies Terezin, at the confluence of the Ohře and Labe rivers. The fortress-village sits on a rolling plain ringed by low hills. It is a place of green meadows, wild flowers, small turreted towns. Churches abound. Their predominant colors are white, black and the distinctive Maria Theresa yellow.

Terezin is one of those fortress-villages that appear charming from a distance, but accumulate ugliness as one nears them. From far away, there is a sense of form—a water tower, high escarpments. A deep trench, once a protective moat, surrounds the village. But the historical truth is that Terezin's military value was like a whore's virtue. It did not exist, and if it did, it would not have been worth taking. Never defended, never invested, it remained for years a moss-covered monument to Austrian *Schlamperei*, a relic of Habsburg trivia.

In outline, the town is a many-pointed star. Across the Ohře stands a second walled unit, the *Kleine Festung*, or Little Fortress. By 1882, both were abandoned as fortifications, but the

At the Borders of the Ghetto by Bedřich Fritta

People at Work by Bedřich Fritta

town continued to house a garrison. The grim multistoried barracks with their lofty attics remained. The checkerboard design of intersecting streets, replete with courts, gates, galleries was preserved. Over all there hovered an odor of decay.

The decision to move the Jews of the Protektorat into Terezin was made at a meeting held on October 10, 1941, in Prague Castle. Heydrich was present; so was Eichmann. "Transport to the ghetto of Terezin would not require much time . . . two or three trains containing a thousand Jews could be sent every day."

A week later the SS officials met again. Plans were refined: "Jews from Bohemia and Moravia will be assembled for evacuation. For this purpose the commander in chief will have completely evacuated all armed forces from Terezin. The Czechs there will be advised to move elsewhere. Fifty or sixty thousand Jews may be comfortably accommodated in Terezin. From there the Jews will go east. . . ."

As early as October of 1941, Terezin's role had been determined. The old folks' home, the camp for privileged Jews, the model ghetto were all secondary facets. And how marvelously it slid into its role! So swiftly did it speed its transports east that a second ghetto, planned for Kyjov in Moravia, was never built!

Terezin suited the Germans for many reasons. It was a fort and could be easily controlled, cheaply guarded. It had store houses, administrative offices. Across the river, the *Kleine Festung* made a superb Gestapo prison, one hoary with precedent. In it, Gavrilo Princip, the assassin of the Archduke Ferdinand, had been imprisoned and had died. Nearby was the rail station of Bohušovice. Another neighboring town, Litoměřice, housed Wehrmacht and SS troops.

With customary attention to detail, the SS ordered the Prague Jewish leaders to recruit a team of experts to convert the Terezin barracks. Suddenly the Jewish officials were filled with optimism. How bad could it really be? The Germans asked for police, postal experts, administrators, financial and economic experts. A little town of their own!

Indeed, the news of Terezin caused many sighs of relief. Already five transports of Czech Jews had been sent to the dreaded East, for work camps in Lodz and Minsk. In these early years, no one knew that "East" meant extermination. But it was distant, cold; far from warm, comfortable Czechoslovakia, where Jews had felt more or less at home since 1076. Good King Vratislav had in 1092 granted them the same rights as German merchants. True, the first pogrom took place in 1096, but the killers were not native Czechs but German crusaders. The Bishop of Prague, Kosmas, denounced the killings, but was ignored.

With the memory of these early shipments eastward imprinted in their minds, the Czech Jews accepted the German invitation to Terezin with a sigh of relief. The first work group, the *Aufbaukommando*, was quickly organized. In addition to the high-level specialists already cited, it included many young, strong, skilled men—mechanics, drivers, construction workers. It comprised 342 men, most of them volunteers. Work at Terezin, they were told, and your families will not go "east."

Then came a characteristic German move. Lieutenant Colonel Dr. Siegfried Seidl, first commandant of Terezin, struck the names of all the "experts" from the list and replaced them with laborers. A shudder went through the Jewish community.

On November 24, 1941, the *Aufbaukommando* left Prague for Terezin. They were the first to occupy the new camp, into which eventually 140,000 would come, and 112,000 die. But this was 1941. No one really believed that Czech Jews would be murdered. These were people whose roots went back to the eleventh century. They worshiped in one of the world's most beautiful synagogues. They owned Steinways and leather-bound libraries. They were teachers, doctors, scientists, artists . . .

One such artist was a member of the *Aufbaukommando*. This was Bedřich Taussig, whose pen name, the one he preferred, was Fritta. Fritta was assigned the job of head draftsman in the construction office, the *Zeichenstube*. The bulk of Fritta's time, and that of his fellow artists, Bloch, Haas and Ungar, and the architect Norbert Troller, was spent creating charts. The Germans were insatiable. They never had enough diagrams, maps, chains of command, little boxes, arrows, lines, rectangles, chart on top of chart. New planning concepts, new routings, new underlings, new bosses. So long as the flow of charts was unimpeded, the SS was content to leave the artists alone. They were a camp élite.

Fritta headed the group, and he seems to have accepted his role with a fatalistic shrug. His wife and his infant son Tomáš accompanied him to Terezin. Troller remembers him as an outgoing, robust, outspoken man. "There was nothing of the shy Bohemian about him," he told me; "he was a solid citizen." In Prague, Fritta had worked as an illustrator, commercial artist and draftsman, and had once taught art classes in his apartment. A former student, Fred Kantor, who was also a member of the *Aufbaukommando*, remembers paying one koruna for an hour of instruction. Fritta did not have many students, perhaps four or five, but he was an enthusiastic teacher.

Bedřich Fritta seems to have brought this enthusiasm to all of his projects. In addition to his paintings and drawings of Terezin, there survives a remarkable children's book by Fritta. It is a primer, dedicated to and created for his son Tomáš, a hand-made limited edition—a single copy, bound by the artist with coarse brown cloth, filled with bright, vivacious drawings, lavishly colored, and captioned in large neat lettering. From this lovely book, little Tomáš learned to read and write. Orphaned by the Nazis, young Fritta was adopted and raised by his father's

44

To Tommy on his third birthday in Terezin—January 22, 1944

(This drawing and the following nine are from Bedřich Fritta's Tomíčkovi.*)*

Tommy is praying.

My mother   My father

This is not a fairy tale. It's true!

And what would you like to be? An engineer?

Or a boxer?

Or a painter?

And also not a general!

But not a businessman, I beg you!

Or a big detective?

friend Leo Haas, and now lives in Israel. Tomáš has kept the book over the years. It is almost painful to study the gay cartoons and simple text. And yet it is reassuring, evidence of the capabilities of the human heart and hand under the vilest conditions. I can think of no bequest from father to son that has ever moved me more.

Terezin grew and the myth inflated. In December of 1941 a second team, the *Arbeitskommando*, arrived to finish preparing the camp for the influx. Officials of the Jewish self-government, the *Judenältester*, also arrived. These included Drs. Jacob Edelstein and Otto Zucker. At this time the camp was barely habitable. Sanitary conditions were appalling, kitchen facilities marginal. Long before the work teams could get material to improve the quarters, the Jews began flooding in. In Prague, they would be "processed" at the Prague Sample Fair. Processing involved a three-day wait during which keys, ration cards, money, personal valuables were turned in. Questionnaires were completed. *Alles in Ordnung.*

Once the Jews were in Terezin, their homes were systematically looted. Anything of value, anything movable was stored in synagogues and Jewish clubhouses. The mass thievery was staggering—778,000 books, 603 pianos (those damned Steinways and Bechsteins again) and 21,000 carpets. Much of this loot was periodically shipped to Germany for the *Winterhilfe*—the Winter Aid Society. The cream of it, the best apartments, the lushest furniture, the fine linens, silver, porcelain, enriched the SS. Carloads of stolen goods were sold, an official letter noted, "at very reasonable prices," to German officials in the Protektorat.

Bereft of possessions, their freedom extirpated, the Jews were herded into Terezin. Living conditions, while never quite so appalling as at Dachau or Buchenwald, were hardly pleasant. A barracks room that had housed ten soldiers was now home for fifty prisoners. In the vast damp, windy storerooms, as many as five hundred Jews would be crammed. There were never enough cots or blankets.

At once—to the shock of most of the internees who had consoled themselves with visions of the *Paradeisghetto*—the usual concentration-camp strictures were invoked: daily work parties; no smoking; a curfew; no letters; it was even forbidden to touch a chimney sweep for good luck. Beatings, torture, confinement in the *Kleine Festung* for infractions were the rule.

Under Seidl's brutal hand the camp was organized. (No doubt our artists' charts were part of this.) Each room had a prisoner chief, each barracks a *Gruppenältester*. A commissariat was set up, as were a labor office, hospital, kitchen. But there was never enough water—for washing, for the clinic, for the cooks. The only vehicles for transport were several creaking old hearses formerly used by the Jewish community of Prague. Again, I hear that spongy laughter in the background. Surely those baroque death wagons were chosen by the Nazis as some sort of joke.

It is noteworthy, too, how the hearse dominated the artists' imaginations. It keeps turning up—an ornate relic, bearer of the dead, but at the same time a reminder of a saner, more orderly world. It is the subject of Fleischmann's sketch called simply *The Hearse,* and can also be discerned in the foreground of his *Theater Performance.* It turns up in the foreground of Bedřich Fritta's painting *Potemkin-Style Shops.* It appears twice in sketches by the woman artist Malvína Schálková—once bearing Terezin children, a second time being hauled through the streets loaded with the day's ration of bread. Leo Haas depicted it at least twice—in *Ghetto-Swingers,* a scene showing the Terezin

Potemkin-style Shops (shops created by the Nazis to deceive the outside world) by Bedřich Fritta

The Hearse by Karel Fleischmann

The Hearse by Bedřich Fritta

Bread Being Delivered by Malvína Schálková

Hearse by Malvína Schálková

Hunger by Leo Haas

Ghetto-Swingers by Leo Haas

jazz band giving a concert while the hearse moves grimly across the foreground, and again in *Hunger*. This was one of the paintings for which Haas and his colleagues were eventually arrested and tortured. It shows Terezin oldsters foraging for food amid garbage heaps; in the background others scramble on the floor of the hearse for leavings from the bread ration.

The menu was unvarying: unsweetened black ersatz coffee and bread for breakfast; watery soup for lunch; soup and bread for dinner. The privileged few fared better. Those who had money in Prague, usually with Christian relatives or friends, could buy food from the guards.

But from the beginning pipe dreams persisted. Illusion fed on illusion; rumors were almost always optimistic. There would be more food, more room; life would have to get better. Then, in January and February of 1942, a few months before Hitler made the decision to annihilate every Jew in Europe, the SS cracked down. Nine men were hanged for petty offenses—an illegal conversation with a wife, a smuggled message. Seven more were hanged in February. (Leo Haas has recorded these scenes with a merciless pen.) A few had been promised leniency if they confessed. They confessed; they were executed anyway. Sixteen lives barely seems worth a turning point at Terezin. From then on, very few believed in the *Reichsaltersheim*.

Also in January of 1942, an event equally terrifying occurred. The first shipments "east" left Terezin. Now every inmate lived in perpetual terror of being transported. The orders came regularly from Berlin; the trainloads chugged slowly out of Bohušovice. As usual, the SS would saddle the Jewish officials, the *Judenältester*, with the job of selecting the transports.

It is instructive to study the manner in which the SS command handled the shipment orders from Berlin. Whim, caprice, cunning—all these inform the Nazi *modus operandi*. It became a game of cat-and-mouse of staggering proportions. The supply

Theater Performance by Karel Fleischmann

In the Attic by Bedřich Fritta

Execution by Leo Haas

of mice was endless. At one time, the aged were exempted from transport. Later, old people were prime selections for the death camps. In the early months, the ill were spared. But in preparation for the famous Red Cross inspection of 1944, an entire TB ward, coughing, spitting skeletons, were hustled off to the gas chambers. Often those with special skills enjoyed a protected status. But even the élite *Aufbaukommando*, the camp cadre, was eventually shipped off to finish its days in Auschwitz, from where only a handful emerged.

By the summer of 1942, Terezin had settled into a deadly rhythm, fulfilling its role as a great reservoir for Central European Jews, a catch basin for the Final Solution. Heydrich had been assassinated; Lidice razed. The camp was almost always crowded. One can experience the foul, oppressive conditions in the barracks by studying Fritta's sketch *In the Attic*. It is all there—the destruction of privacy, the absence of minimal comfort, the despair of the aged and blind, the eroding communal life, the shortages of air, space, sanitation.

Late in 1942 numerous German Jews arrived at Terezin. Many were older people, invalids, pensioners, war veterans. In Berlin, Munich and Nürnberg, Nazi officials had reassuringly told these poor dupes that they were very lucky people. They were made to sign faked contracts for "accommodation in the ghetto for old persons." Cheery SS men acted like travel agents, describing the splendid bill of fare, the soft goosedown beds, the concerts and theater. Old Jews surrendered their last Reichsmark, and gossiped happily. In their euphoria they packed top hats, frock coats and lace dresses. There is a memorable painting by Dr. Karel Fleischmann, *First Night of New Arrivals*, that eerily evokes what these deceived oldsters must have felt on arriving at the camp. Almost in the attitudes of vacationers reclining in deck chairs—one man sports a rakish hat—the new prisoners lounge on their valises. But they already have the look

First Night of New Arrivals by Karel Fleischmann

of walking dead, of people stupefied by some horrible truth.

Elderly Berlin Jews, elegant *Damen* and *Herren*, demanded rooms with a view of the lake! Had not the nice SS officers in Berlin promised it to them? The guards promptly relieved them of their possessions (there went the top hats and parasols) and shoved them into filthy attics or dank underground chambers. Soon they were ravaged by hunger, diarrhea, consumption. So much for Theresienbad, the health spa.

Overcrowding exacted a terrible toll. The daily death rate hit 130. *Judenältester* Edelstein reported this to Commandant Seidl, who responded, "The clock is going right."

Corpses accumulated and were at first buried in coffins; then in mass graves. But the cemetery was too close to the Ohře River. When it overflowed, moldering bodies were unearthed and floated downstream. Again, the Germans betrayed a strange finickiness, a reluctance to let anyone know that they actually killed people. A crematorium was built, and the dead were committed to·the oven. It was capable of burning 190 bodies per diem.

Meanwhile, mass annihilation proceeded in the East. Terezin had sent eighteen thousand people to the gas chambers by October of 1942. Yet the myth of the model ghetto persisted. "Shops" were opened. There was a food store where the only item on sale was a kind of tongue-burning paste, an ersatz mustard. (Laughter again?) There was a clothing store where one might buy back his own confiscated pants. There was a luggage store that sold the valises of those who had gone east to their death. The town was beautified; a café was opened, complete with a first-rate jazz combo. A newspaper was begun, but the SS prudently ordered it discontinued after Stalingrad.

But the most astonishing flowering of communal life in Terezin was the cultural program that developed under abominable circumstances. It seems incredible that people who had to

Vanity Show by Bedřich Fritta

The Café by Bedřich Fritta

struggle for an extra slice of bread or rancid horse meat, people sleeping in crowded, drafty quarters, subjected to abuse and humiliation, living under the constant threat of transport and death, could have undertaken such remarkable enterprises—concerts, cabarets, operas, lectures, *vernissages*. It would appear the SS had no objection—provided nothing was political, didactic, in any way a commentary. And of course "horror propaganda" was absolutely forbidden.

But *Carmen* was fine. I'm told the performance was an excellent one. I even met the woman who created Carmen's rose—in the Terezin handicrafts factory. Even more thrilling was *The Bartered Bride*, which had its premiere on November 28, 1942. The indefatigable Schachter rehearsed his chorus of peasant girls in a freezing cellar. An ancient Bechstein, which had somehow found its way to Terezin, was moved to the boys' school. When the first bars, *Proč bychom se netěšili* (Why should we not rejoice?), rang out, the audience wept freely, then applauded. *The Bartered Bride* was performed thirty-five times!

Arnošt Weiss, an engineer and an amateur violinist, recalls a humorous incident that dramatizes the pervasiveness of music in Terezin, the way it eased the lives of so many prisoners. Weiss was whistling in the latrine one day when an elderly man stopped him. "Young man," he asked, "do you know what you are whistling?"

Weiss replied that he did, that it was Beethoven's "Razumovsky" Quartet No. 1. The older man embraced him and identified himself as Herr Freudenthal, former concertmaster of the Ústí Opera. Freudenthal then proceeded to whistle the first part of the quartet, while young Weiss whistled and hummed the other three, taking up first one, then another. As he noted wryly years later, "That was my first quartet playing in Terezin."

The Theater by Otto Ungar

Ghetto Scene by Leo Haas

The "Café" by Leo Haas

Karel Ančerl, later chief conductor of the Prague Philharmonic Orchestra, was also active in musical production in Terezin. He organized a group of distinguished musicians. Among their favorite selections were Dvořák's "Serenade for Strings," and the "Meditation" based on the St. Wenceslas Chorale by Suk.

Ančerl has written:

> . . . *it is hardly possible to imagine the quality of the orchestra which scarcely existed for a year; in any case, one thing was revealed to me, that the power of music is so great that it draws every human being possessing a heart and an open mind into its realm, enabling him to bear the hardest hours of his life.*

Other attempts to create an approximation of Jewish life were actively encouraged. For example, a ghetto bank was opened. The worthless currency was in denominations of one, two, five, ten, fifty and one hundred koruny. It was paid as wages or given for hard currency the prisoners might receive from the outside. The valueless bills bear on their face a cartoon of Moses carrying the tablets. Another German joke?

But for all these "softening" measures, there were repeated hints that all Jews trapped in the Nazi web—whether Czech or German or Polish—were doomed. In the summer of 1943 a trainload of Jewish children arrived at Terezin. The children had been routed to Czechoslovakia after internment at a death camp. There were about 1,300 children in the group, ranging in age from six to fifteen. Under SS guns, this troop of small, starving ghosts was paraded through the ghetto to the delousing station. Many were barefoot.

Stumbling through the streets of Terezin in rags, their eyes haunted, they were unlike anything the prisoners had yet seen. At the delousing station, some children saw the word "gas." At once they began to weep and shriek, refusing to enter. The SS had to drag them in. Later, some of them revealed their story. They were from Bialystok in Poland. The SS had shot their mothers and fathers before their eyes. For some reason—one of those capricious decisions that color the Final Solution—the children were spared. Within a few months after their arrival, most of them died of typhus. They were the last transport to arrive at Terezin in 1943, and they were chilling evidence that Europe was on its way to becoming *judenrein*.

The incident of the Bialystok children leads me to the post-terror analyses of Jewish behavior. Did they submit too readily? Do they share a little of the guilt for being such cooperative victims? Were they concerned so much with survival that they refused to die with honor? The arguments are well known by now, and I am not certain that anything will be gained by reviewing them. It has always seemed to me that the overwhelming, crushing, relentless, diabolically cunning manner in which the Germans went about collecting, disarming, and finally murdering Jews precluded anything but the feeblest of protests. Urban dwellers, aliens in their own lands, people with no place to hide and damned little sympathy in the outside world, people with close family ties, always pleading, accommodating, making deals with Christian overlords. The wonder to me is not that so few fought back, but that *any* were able to.

I keep thinking of Fritta's old people in the attic or Fleischmann's new arrivals, and the wide-eyed ghost children of Bialystok, and I have great difficulty envisioning them at the throat of some fat, healthy blond SS sergeant. Professor Bruno Bettelheim argues with great force that had some of the stronger Jews possessed better "informed" hearts, they would not have succumbed to the death wish, and would have forsaken their deceptively safe hiding places, their attempts at "business as usual," and opted for flight and resistance. It is a persuasive argument, but I keep wondering what I would have done. A survivor of

79

Terezin, a young man who served with the *Aufbaukommando*, told me how ashamed he was that they never tried to escape. "The first day at Terezin," he said, "they assembled us, over three hundred young guys, in the square, and two SS men read the orders to us. No guns. No dogs. No walls. We could have jumped then and run away. But it never occurred to us." He paused a moment. "But why should we have done it? Everything looked pretty good then. So we didn't do anything. And later— well, later it was too late."

Perhaps it is also too late to start analyzing why the Jews did not resist. This question, it seems to me, clouds a much more important one. Why did the Germans—let us forget those unarmed friendless Jews for the moment—behave as they did? What I crave are explanations, theories, motivational research on the subject of the *murderers*, not the victims. Criminologists do not spend their lives examining the motives and behavior of the victims of crime. It is the criminal whose acts are deemed worthy of analysis. Dr. Mengele, the SS guards who shoved nude women into the chambers, Himmler, the helpful Ukrainians in the snowy fields, heaping high the bodies of children—these are the people whose acts seem to me to demand closer study.

I've already mentioned the manner in which the Nazi crimes elude ordinary language. Certainly the same problem confronted the artists. Leo Haas' drawings of the SS men, the commandants and underlings, while bitter and satiric, seem to me to scratch only the surface. They are very sharp indeed, but they seem somehow to miss; maybe certain varieties of evil cannot be recorded—in the manner in which witches and vampires are said to be immune to mirrors. Haas' depictions of his jailers in his execution sketches, in *Camp Commander*, and *The Coming of a Transport*, are shrewd, keenly observed works—but only part of the story.

Camp Commander by Leo Haas

The Transport Has Arrived by Leo Haas

He can't be blamed. He is dealing with events that to a great extent are still inexplicable. We can draw up the usual historian's list—German nationalism, Versailles, fear and hatred of Bolshevism, two thousand years of sanctioned Jew-hating, economic expansion—and none will satisfactorily explain the naked people at the edge of the pit. How many dead children does it take, after all, to secure a favorable balance of trade?

To return to the history of Terezin. By the end of 1943, the camp was admirably fulfilling its purposes—a false front to show the world, a pool for the doomed. The new SS commandant, Anton Burger, was a perfectionist. He was a fanatic for lists and charts. It had come to his attention that there had been fifty-five verified escapes from the camp. Moreover, he suspected that the *Judenältester* were falsifying the population reports. Both circumstances were intolerable.

Burger ordered a census. It took place on a misty, drizzling day, November 17, 1943. All forty thousand prisoners were marched to a muddy field, a low meadow lying between mountains. There this great host stood all day, without food or water, with no toilets, bending, weeping, murmuring, fainting. Planes circled overhead; machine guns bristled on the mountains, as a lunatic attempt at a full count of heads was begun. Toward evening the prisoners' endurance crumpled, and panic broke out. Children shrieked; women fainted. The old and ill collapsed. Many died. From seven in the morning until midnight, the census went on, and it established nothing at all—merely that there were approximately forty thousand people in the camp. When, after midnight, the Jews were allowed to stagger back to the camp, over three hundred corpses remained on the muddy field. A painting by Leo Haas, *The Count-Out*, has recorded the event.

The horror of the mad census was still etched in the prisoners' minds when, in the spring of 1944, the great beautification program got under way.

Terezin, once and for all, would emerge as the *Paradeisghetto*, the Jews' own little town.

The beautification plan coincided with the arrival of a new camp commandant, SS Captain Karl Rahm, an Austrian. A member of the Viennese *lumpen* middle class, Rahm, according to some survivors, was not the worst of the commandants. "A dog who barks rather than bites," was *Judenältester* Eppstein's opinion of him.

To Rahm was entrusted this renovation of the old fortress. He pursued it with such frenzy that one gets the impression that as Nazi crimes grew more bestial, as the corpses were dragged in increasing numbers from the gas chambers, as the mass graves overflowed, the lie of the *Paradeisghetto* had to be fortified. Again, we must ask why. Out of a sense of guilt? As an escape hatch, a bit of insurance? And again, one must conclude that most Nazis could not have been terribly proud of their villainy, not completely convinced of their absolute right to murder. Had that been the case, their news agencies should have distributed, with great enthusiasm, those photographs of nude women waiting for death, the heaps of dead. But there is no record of press handouts, syndicated halftones, newsreel clips about the murder camps. These were crimes committed in the dark, deeds of midnight. A great screen is erected in front of the smoking furnaces; all bloody hands are sworn to silence. Drunkards, braggarts, unreliables were carefully weeded out of the death factories; the less talk, the better. Hans and Fritz pulled the trigger, released the clouds of Zyklon B, but always with a furtive glance over their epaulets.

In moments of stupefied bewilderment, I can picture myself sitting opposite a panel of former SS men—lumpish, aging gray-blond fellows with rosy cheeks and the pale flat eyes of the northern European. Like a shlemiel I keep asking—Why, why? How could you? Aren't you human beings? Don't you have kids of your own? Didn't they teach you differently in school? What did the priest say in church? I get no answers. Just those flat smiles.

Long ago I stared at a newspaper photograph of a Jewish family in some German city, an ordinary family snapped in mid-passage down a cobbled street. A short bespectacled father in a lumpy topcoat and a felt hat, an ill-formed mother, and two scrawny kids in leggings, carrying schoolbags. I had the feeling that the nervous parents were convoying the children to school to keep them from getting beaten. They appear to have halted suddenly, as if arrested by a curse, a taunt, an obscenity. They are frozen forever in my mind, those four defenseless Jews. Six or seven years later, I suppose, they helped feed the furnaces. But at the moment I saw them, they were a quartet of lost souls on a street of those trim German shops, leafy trees. Behind them, in the middle distance of the photograph, are three storm troopers, overfed cabbageheads in quasi-military uniforms. They are grinning. Wide thin smiles. I suppose I was fourteen or fifteen when I saw the picture. It haunts me to this day. What, what in the name of God are they smiling about?

This twisted sense of humor seems to have colored the German campaign to beautify Terezin. The camp was proving an enormous success on all counts—as a showplace, as a marshaling area, as a labor force. Rahm gloried in it; he pushed the refurbishment with vigor, imagination. So what if hundreds starved and died of typhus? Outside, the casern walls were freshly painted. Flowers bloomed on trimmed lawns. The cultural life flourished. Even a few fences came down. In the evening the strains of American jazz issued from the café.

What many of the prisoners suspected was behind the great

85

The Count-Out by Leo Haas

Registration by Karel Fleischmann

cleanup was soon confirmed. The International Red Cross was soon to arrive at Terezin to see for themselves how Jews were being treated. Rahm was determined to pass inspection. New linen was issued to the hospital. The nurses were given fresh uniforms. It was a far cry from the haphazard medical arrangements of the previous year. As dedicated as the Jewish doctors had been, most of them could not cope with the overcrowding, the lack of medicine, the unsanitary conditions. Mrs. Ahlfeld-Schlesinger, a native of Cologne who spent two years in Terezin, recalls working as a nurse for an elderly physician, Dr. Martha Wygodzinsky. Dr. Wygodzinsky, a tiny, white-haired lady in her seventies, had been known in her native Berlin as "the angel of Nordens." She had run a volunteer charity hospital for unwed mothers. In Terezin, she made her rounds on swollen, crippled feet, ill with diarrhea and the typhus that would eventually kill her. But that was the old Terezin; the new one would be sterile, spotless.

Of course, the beautification plan was selective. Community buildings—the hospital, the children's quarters—were scrubbed and painted. So were the VIP barracks. But the vast three-story buildings with their drafty attics were barely touched. Evidently the SS would decide what the Red Cross could see and what they could not.

Even the nature of the transports was affected by the impending Red Cross visit. For the sake of "the beauty of the camp," all orphans were abruptly shipped "east." (We must keep in mind that of 15,000 children who passed through Terezin, about 150 lived.) Those suffering from tuberculosis were also sent off to Auschwitz. Rahm took a personal hand at supervising the shipments. He was careful to exempt anyone who looked healthy, especially pretty girls. Just before the Red Cross group was to arrive, in June, a final transport of 7,500 was ordered. A frenzy seized the prisoners. Inmates hid, schemed, bargained for their lives. It was only by a superhuman effort that Rahm was able to meet the quota. The camp was now ready.

The commission arrived on June 23, 1944. Its members included a man from the Danish Ministry of Foreign Affairs (there were some four hundred Danish Jews in Terezin, all with privileged status), the Chairman of the Danish Red Cross, and representatives of the Danish Red Cross in Berlin. There were also a party of top-ranking Nazi officials from Berlin and Prague. As the guests drove up to the main gate, they were greeted by Captain Rahm and his aides, all in civilian clothing. Jack boots and side arms were *verboten*.

Rahm had done his job brilliantly. He led the inspectors through spotless streets, houses bright in pastel shades, an adorable Maria Theresa village. On cue, a squad of singing Jewish girls, shouldering rakes, marched off to their gardening. White-gloved bakers unloaded fresh bread into a fake store. At another shop, fresh vegetables were displayed—for the first and last time. In the community center, Terezin's orchestra played Mozart. As the inspectors approached a soccer field, a goal was scored according to script.

One of the shabbiest deceits was acted out inside the ghetto bank. There, Herr Direktor Friedmann, puffing a cigar, offering cigarettes to the visitors, explained the importance of the bank in community life. (He did not explain that the notes with Moses' noble head were worthless.) Friedmann's speech was a crisp summary of currency circulation, the cash reserve, the "evacuation fund"—and it was meaningless. This particular bit of insanity even turned up at the Nürnberg trials, where several defendants cited the Terezin bank as evidence of their compassionate treatment of the Jews!

It was a memorable day, that warm June 23. The band played in the square. Children in clean clothing rode a merry-go-round. *Judenältester* Eppstein wore a pressed black suit and was chauffered around by an SS man who, the day before, had kicked and beaten him. Today he opened the door of Eppstein's car, and bowed.

Naturally some aspects of Terezin life were screened from the Red Cross. No one saw the crowded barracks filled with the aged, the ill, the dying. Nor was anyone shown the storehouses filled with goods stolen from the Jews.

After a relaxing day, the men from the Red Cross departed. As far as is known, they were satisfied with what they saw. Conceivably some of them went to Terezin predisposed to believe everything. It should not surprise us.

The fantastic success of the Terezin hoax now emboldened the SS to elaborate on it. There were no limits to the good will that could be reaped from this small town. It was decided that a documentary film about the camp should be made, a film that would prove to the world that the Jews were being treated far better than they deserved. If Germany, through some miscalculation, lost the war, it would make for excellent insurance.

Kurt Gerron, a Dutch Jew, and a former film director for UFA, was a prisoner at Terezin. One day in the summer of 1944 he was summoned to Rahm's office and ordered to produce and direct a film to be called *The Führer Presents the Jews with a City*. Gerron was flabbergasted. He conferred with the Jewish leaders, and they told him he could not refuse. So, with the help of a Berlin manufacturer and amateur writer named Greifenhagen, he began a script. The connecting tissue, the leitmotiv of his effort was water—the rivers, bathtubs, faucets, showers, irrigation ditches. Evidently Berlin liked this aqueous view of Terezin, and approval was given to start filming. A team of documentary cameramen was sent from Berlin, and under watchful SS guards the project got under way.

A prisoner who worked as Gerron's assistant later wrote that only a handful of people were willing to appear in the film.

The majority of the fifty thousand Jews would drift away when cameras appeared, find excuses to avoid the enactments of camp life. There was an additional problem. Berlin had decreed that only prisoners who *looked* like Jews could appear. They were to be hook-nosed, dark-haired, dark-eyed, and preferably furtive in manner. This presented a problem for the assistant director. Terezin was filled with blue-eyed, blond-haired Jews, and they were automatically excluded. A sequence showing a track meet presented a crisis—the woman high-jump champion of Czecho-slovakia, a Jew, was forbidden to participate. She had blond hair.

The "bank" was filmed. So was the post office, where prison-ers received fake packages. On the riverbank, a swimming meet was held. The national high-diving champion performed. Just out of range were boats filled with armed SS men in the event any of the contestants decided to swim to freedom.

For days the cameras whirred, the lights were focused on the stunned prisoners. A meeting of the Jewish Council was moved from a dingy room in the Magdeburg Barracks to a bright room in the gymnasium. Herr Eppstein addressed his col-leagues, but no sound was recorded. His speech was dubbed in Berlin. To this day no one knows what the tormented man was forced to say. (This filming took place in July, 1944. Two months later, Dr. Eppstein, a brave man who faced up to the SS with courage and humor, was shot dead at Rahm's orders. Rahm had long wanted to be rid of him. The circumstances of his death were as follows: at Rahm's order, relayed by an underling, Epp-stein went to a location normally off limits to get some sacks. Rahm saw him there, accused him of attempting escape, and had him hustled off to the *Kleine Festung*, where he was executed. The dog had a bite.)

Gerron's film grew with a life of its own. Firemen in new uni-forms put out a fire. One day food rations were tripled for the

The Evening Soup by Karel Fleischmann

Israel and Sarah by Bedřich Fritta

filming. In the gym, *The Tales of Hoffmann* was performed. An especially touching scene was filmed at the VIP barracks. Like misty ghosts from a Europe long dead, Rabbi Baeck, Field Marshal von Sommer, the Mayor of Lyons, M. Meyer, and several Czech ministers participated in a pleasant garden party, chatting, sipping coffee.

When a train bearing Jewish children from Holland arrived, Rahm himself was there to welcome them, lifting the youngsters from the wagons. It was dutifully recorded. Then, abruptly, the filming ended. The technicians were ordered back to Berlin. Gerron was discharged. Band concerts were terminated; dancing was forbidden. The camp slipped back into its cruel, starved routine. The old and the ill died and were cremated. The same children whom Rahm took from the train were sent to Auschwitz.

As for the film, it was never shown, and was apparently never even edited. Several still photographs made from it do survive, and must have been distributed at one time. One shows a meeting of the *Judenältester*. Dr. Eppstein stands at the long table addressing his colleagues. His face is strained, as if the horrid fake in which he is forced to take part weighs heavily on his mind. His mouth is drawn, his eyes are frowning, and a perplexed vertical crease separates his eyebrows. Dr. Murmelstein, his aide and successor, squints up at him, he too surfeited with disbelief. On Eppstein's left breast pocket is a cloth Jewish star. The Nazis left a morsel of truth in the film.

Both the Red Cross incident and the documentary film underscore the Nazis' efforts to create and enforce the image of Terezin as the "good" concentration camp, to impress upon the world that they were treating Jews with kindness and understanding and that the Jews were ungrateful wretches. They are

94

the reverse side of the coins of truth minted by the artists of Terezin.

At no time did the Germans' regard for their offended persons manifest itself in more terrible fashion than in "the incident of the artists." In time and in import, the artists' affair is closely tied to the Red Cross inspection of June, 1944, and the documentary film project that followed it. In simplest terms, the SS command, all the way up to Eichmann, entertained a shuddering fear that all the sedulously constructed lies about Terezin would be shattered by a sheaf of drawings and paintings.

It is difficult to envision these lords of the earth in their black boots, with their side arms and bludgeons, their unlimited power to maim, torture and murder, these men of infallible cunning, with their capacity to deceive, to lie, to escape retribution, rendered furious and fearful by a handful of artists. Could Otto Ungar, frail and frightened, really have been that much of a threat to them? Or Fritta? Or Leo Haas?

A few weeks after the departure of the inspection group— it was the middle of July, 1944—a group of Terezin artists were summoned to the Jewish Council in the Magdeburg Barracks. Four men, all of them members of the privileged *Zeichenstube*, reported. They were Bedřich Fritta, Felix Bloch, Otto Ungar and Leo Haas. Dr. Otto Zucker, Eppstein's deputy, informed them that they were to report to the office of SS Commandant Rahm the next morning. What was it all about? Dr. Zucker did not know. But he did suggest, somewhat ominously, that they take along a warm coat and warm underclothing. The cellar of the SS office, he told them, could get rather cold. This suggested to them a long period of detention, and they attempted to draw

95

Daytime scenes by Karel Fleischmann

Zucker out. At length he conceded that there was the possibility they might be detained "for a while." But he felt that everything would turn out all right, that they would not be harmed.

The following morning, July 17, Ungar, Fritta, Bloch and Haas reported to the SS office. Lieutenant Haindl, Rahm's second-in-command, they were told, would handle the investigation. As they awaited Haindl, two more prisoners appeared at the office. One was a young architect from Brno, Norbert Troller, who also worked at drafting, and had made some portraits of Terezin children. Troller recalls that it was a hot day; he was wearing shorts and sandals when he was told to go to the SS headquarters. The sixth prisoner was not an artist, but an elderly merchant from the city of Náchod named František Strass.

At the sight of Strass' lean, white-haired figure, the artists grew uneasy. Zucker's comforting words were forgotten. Ordered to remain silent by the guards, they exchanged fretful glances. Ungar was the most troubled. When the guards left for a moment, Fritta and Haas tried to cheer him up.

But they were just as worried as Ungar. And their fears were grounded in the presence of Herr Strass. This Strass was a wealthy man, an insatiable art collector. He had Christian relatives by marriage in Prague, who had been transmitting to him, via the Czech police, food, tobacco and money. Imprisonment was no deterrent to Strass' love for art. With the goods and cash he got from outside, he proceeded to build a collection, trading cigarettes and marmalade and biscuits for their works. Over a period of years he had accumulated a huge store of sketches, water colors, pen-and-ink drawings. This trade in art was not unusual in Terezin. Nor was it frowned upon by the Germans. Perhaps it was illegal, but it was overlooked. Mr. Greta Pearlman has kindly shown me several water-color landscapes by Dr.

Fleischmann and a Professor Stein, which she purchased with bread or a slice of horse meat during the months she worked in the kitchen. Stein, she told me, had some paintings that he refused to sell—no matter how hungry he was. Mrs. Martha Klein von Peci has in her possession drawings of ghetto life by the Dutch artist Josef Spier, which she purchased in Terezin. Fred Kantor, who was in the *Aufbaukommando*, made little paintings of the prisoners' bunks which he sold for cigarettes. Thus, the art trade was not uncommon, and was not a secret.

But all the paintings to which I have just referred were of an innocuous and neutral nature. They were mainly landscapes, portraits, pleasant pictures of ghetto life. Indeed, Spier's drawings were so attractive that they were tacked upon the walls of the children's ward. On at least one occasion, the Germans had permitted a *vernissage*, at which Fritta, Ungar and the others exhibited their works. Needless to say, they were works that could have offended no one. It was a memorable event; a young Prague cellist, Kurt Heller, played Bach.

Why, then, this sudden excitement over the artists?

The explanation lies in the *secret* works of the painters, the works created clandestinely, the works that told the truth about Terezin. František Strass had purchased dozens of them. Some he had hidden; others he had smuggled out to his relatives in Prague. Through no fault of his, other than his avidity as a collector, he was to bring disaster to the artists and to himself.

The artists were a favored group. Some, like Fritta, had come to Terezin with the cadre, the *Aufbaukommando*. He and possibly a few of the others were told they were exempted from transport because of their skills. Fritta later became the head of the drafting office. He built up his team carefully—Ungar, Haas, a young man named Petr Kien, Bloch, and a Viennese named Pock. Compared to the general run of work in Terezin, their duties were light and pleasant. They spent most of their time working on charts, blueprints, posters. Leo Haas, a superb cartoonist and caricaturist, remembers turning out posters addressed to children—*Children, don't do that!*—to enforce cleanliness.

In their office, they had access to paper, ink, paints, pens, brushes. The Germans supplied these liberally—anything to encourage the production of charts. With materials available, with spare time, the artists were allowed to engage in purely esthetic work, provided it was not critical or of a political nature. The Germans had a word for such works—*Greuelpropaganda*—horror propaganda.

But soon the artists were working secretly to record the truth about Terezin. The leaders in this work appear to have been Haas and Fritta. They even had a password to encourage their subversive paintings. "Write this down, Kisch!" they would whisper to one another. (I gather that this Czech expression corresponds to "Tell it like it is.") The covert works were created at night in the barracks; on the job when the SS were not around; in crowds, on small sketch pads.

Fritta and Haas were natural leaders in the effort to depict the truth of Terezin. Fritta had always been political and anti-German. Fred Kantor, who studied with him in Prague, remembers him with affection. "He had guts," Kantor said; "he always came out and said what he believed." Leo Haas had already begun compiling a sketchbook of prison life while at Nisko, where he had been a forced laborer. He had smuggled these into Terezin, and intended to pursue this "cycle" of prison pictures.

So while the Red Cross teams were paraded through scrubbed streets, and Goebbels ranted about Jews who drank coffee and ate cake in Terezin, the artists recorded the realities. If we want to know the truth of the Terezin café, we must study Fritta's painting of it. We see it in hard, simple lines: the band,

Mass Burial by Leo Haas

the curtained windows, customers nursing their demitasses, the waitress. But there is something else. We see bleak faces, starved bodies, a sense of forced acting amid death and disease.

How could anyone accept the myth of the *Paradeisghetto* after studying Fritta's *Going to Work*? Between the inward sloping walls of the prison, he depicts a sea of hungry, haunted faces, eyes wide with terror and despair. The isolation of camp life has rarely been shown so starkly, so movingly. One harbors the hope that some who took the Red Cross tour on June 23 might have one day seen Fritta's pictures. What would they have said about *Dwellings for the Feeble-Minded?* Or *The Coming of a Transport* —which to me, at least, is his most powerful work? I know of few pictures that more eloquently and poignantly express what must have been the sense of utter desolation, abandonment and imminent death than this simple pen-and-ink sketch. Across the open square stretches a dark line of new arrivals. They are seen as a jagged, misshapen silhouette. A cold rain slants down on them. In the foreground rises a single gnarled tree—for even nature is deformed in this cold hell. Beyond loom the gloomy three-storied barracks that will be home for these doomed Jews, people so recently secure and warm in apartments in Prague and Ostrava and Brno. It is a chilling, spare and truthful work, Fritta at his best. And it is no wonder the Germans did not want the world to see his pictures.

I suspect that Haas' drawings probably infuriated them even more. He is a most political man, a caricaturist and cartoonist with a merciless, biting pen. I have already referred to his bold depictions of his jailers. But he was also compassionate; his works are moral statements of a high order. *The Old and the Ill, Mass Burial* and *Expecting the Worst* are among his finest impressions of ghetto life—wrenching, sorrowful works, they are nonetheless possessed of a certain courage, a sense of outrage that will not succumb.

Going to Work by Bedřich Fritta

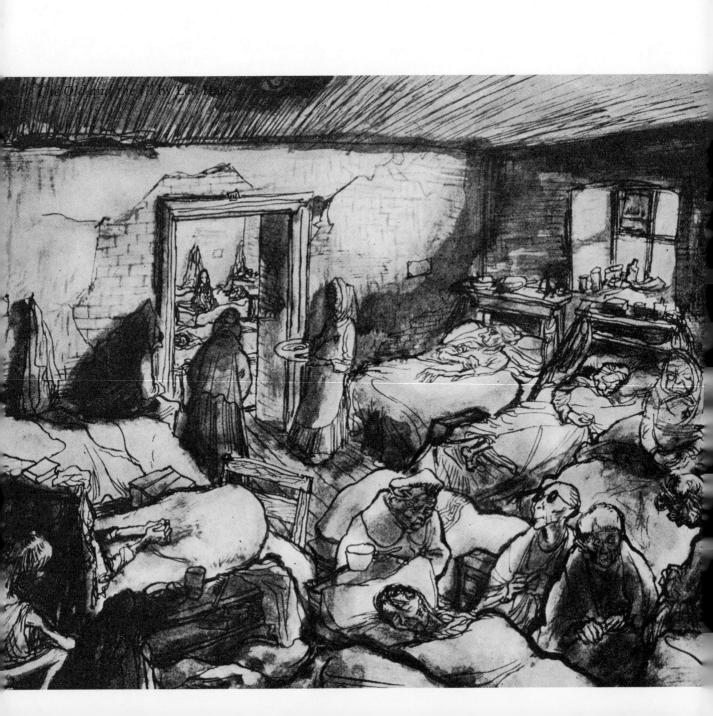

The Old and the Ill by Lea Haas

Dwellings for the Feeble-Minded by Bedřich Fritta

Expecting the Worst by Leo Haas

As the artists awaited interrogation, it occurred to them that Strass' collection was surely no secret to the SS. In March, there had been a lightning search of Strass' barracks, and some drawings had been ripped from the old man's mattress. Norbert Troller has told me that the Nazis raised an enormous fuss at the time. "It seemed far out of proportion to the number and nature of the pictures," the architect recalled. "Most of them were not at all critical." In time, the SS appeared to drop its investigation of the artists, with a warning to Strass to stop his trade in pictures. About the same time, Dr. Eppstein was cautioned that the discovery of the paintings in Strass' mattress had created "a very serious situation." There were hints that the artists were ungrateful scoundrels and that they would be watched closely from now on.

But the March investigation was dropped. All hands were too busy polishing the camp for the Red Cross. Little attention was paid the artists until July 17, when they were assembled in the SS headquarters. Haas began speculating to himself as to why they had been summoned. His conclusions were not encouraging. Strass, he knew, had hidden only a few pictures in his bed. The bulk of them had been smuggled out of Terezin by two Czech guards, brothers named Prikryl. Rumors had come back to the camp that some of Strass' paintings had been sent out of Czechoslovakia, notably to Switzerland. Haas recalled that he, Fritta and Ungar had been overjoyed when they heard the report. They had turned ever more industriously to their secret works. They knew they were running a grave risk, but it was worth it.

Switzerland was the home of the International Red Cross. If somehow their paintings could reach the IRC, perhaps the lie of Terezin might be exposed. At least they could hope so. There were other glimmers of hope. One rumor said that some of the Danish inspectors were dubious of the Potemkin Village; one man had asked searching questions, almost as if he had been briefed beforehand. Was it possible he had seen Fritta's *Quarters of the Aged* or Haas' *Transport to the East?* The rumor was sufficient to hearten the artists; it was also sufficient to throw the Germans into a frenzy. So Haas reasoned, as they sat in silence in the cold basement. The raid on Strass' barracks; the inspection; the Gerron film; a report that Eichmann had learned of the smuggled paintings—all these indicated the inevitable confrontation. Mythopoeic Terezin could not be threatened with the truth.

Haas had other reasons to be fearful. Following the Red Cross inspection, the SS had begun to crack down. Most prisoners were filled with despair. Most of them understood that transport meant death, that Auschwitz was no mere labor camp. As Rabbi Leo Baeck noted: "Perhaps the Commission knew the real conditions, but it looked as if they did not want to know the truth. The effect on our morale was devastating. We felt forgotten and forsaken."

The rabbi was correct. The International Commission had submitted a laudatory report to the Red Cross in Stockholm. Terezin was a comfortable community, not a filthy ghetto. (In fairness to one Danish commission member, Dr. Frantz Hvass of the Danish Foreign Ministry, his role in this affair should be recorded. Dr. Hvass claimed that he deliberately exaggerated his praise of the camp so that the Germans, who were known to respond angrily to criticism, would allow the Danes to continue sending food and medicine to Terezin.)

If the Germans were pleased, the Jews, as indicated in Rabbi Baeck's mournful comment, were shattered. They knew that there was no hope. The world had been deceived; the Nazis could move ahead with a systematic extermination of every Jew in Terezin. That fall, transports were increased. It was the time of the infamous "family camp" of Birkenau. (One of these autum-

Quarters of the Aged by Bedřich Fritta

Transport to the East by Leo Haas

nal transports is worthy of special note. Dr. Zucker's innocent widow—the official had himself been gassed at Auschwitz after having been promised the job of "work camp manager"—organized a transport of Terezin wives and children. They were issued "special permits" to join their husbands and fathers at Birkenau. On arrival, the entire transport of women and children was executed in the chambers. Crematorium No. 1 was found littered with the "special permits" Lieutenant Colonel Eichmann had personally approved as an act of kindness.)

It is against this morbid background that the arrests of the artists must be viewed. The Germans, for all their successful deceptions, were growing uneasy. Throughout the concentration camp network, Jews were becoming restive. There were rumors of rebellion, mutiny. Now that most Jews expected the worst, they might resort to violence. Rahm, at his trial in Vienna, testified that he was fearful of a repetition of the Warsaw Ghetto uprising. Precautions had to be taken. Jews who had served as German, Austrian or Czech army officers were shipped out.

The artists, as evidenced by their horror propaganda, were also viewed as troublemakers. It was all of a piece; all part of the implementation of the Final Solution. At any rate, Haas reflected, as they waited, he had had the foresight to hide many of his paintings. With the help of a fellow prisoner named Beck, a Czech engineer, he had pried open a wall and hidden many works within the paneling. "I did not forget to leave some unimportant drawings lying about," Haas later wrote, "so that if there were another search by the Gestapo, I could stop the mouths of the wolves." Fritta and some of his friends located a large tin case in which they deposited any pictures that might make trouble for him. They buried it in a farmyard. All these hidden works of Fritta and Haas survived the war.

After what seemed an interminable wait, the artists were herded into the office of Commandant Rahm. As they entered,

Haas and Fritta, perhaps the boldest of the group, had the sensation that they might be able to handle the thick-headed Viennese. But to their dismay they saw that Rahm would be a minor figure at the inquiry. This was no low-level routine investigation. All Ungar's fears seemed justified: the affair had attracted the cream of the SS.

Rahm, a bit subdued, was present. But he was outranked by three other SS officers, men who dealt at the highest echelon in Jewish matters. One was Captain Moes, "the bird of death." He was the man reputed to have been responsible for the final massacres at Bergen-Belsen. Also present was SS Captain Hans Günther, Eichmann's "referent" in Prague. This Günther was the son of the Nazi party anthropologist Professor F. K. Günther. It was an unusually talented family. A second brother, Rolf, also an SS officer, was one of the first Nazis to be entrusted with the secret of the gas chambers. On a trip to Lublin in 1942, he brought with him one hundred kilos of prussic acid, used to manufacture Zyklon B. A colleague recalled Rolf Günther warning him: "This is one of the most secret matters . . . anybody who talks about it will be shot immediately."

Rahm, Moes, Günther. The fourth inquisitor was Eichmann. He sat quietly behind Rahm's desk, a rather slight man, thin, pale, dark-haired, with those oddly glittering eyes, Lieutenant Colonel Karl Adolf Eichmann, head of the Jewish Office of the Gestapo's Internal Security Bureau.

Haas had seen Eichmann before, at the Nisko labor camp. He regarded him as an elusive, complex man, not the normal run of SS brute. And now Eichmann lived up to Haas' estimate of him. Opening the questioning, he did not shout or bully or threaten the artists. In a conciliatory manner, Eichmann began to speak. He was offended by what the artists had done. A decent man, he had been betrayed by ingrates. He emphasized to the artists that he had nothing but the most humane intentions where Jews were concerned. What better example than the happy ghetto of Terezin? And what had they done to repay him? Slander, lies, communist propaganda! Those disgusting, deceitful pictures!

When Eichmann finished his opening comments, a model of aggrieved sensibilities, the questioning was taken up by Hans Günther and Rahm. These two also adopted a discursive tone. Like parvenu collectors, eager dilettantes, they tried to impress the artists with their interest in painting. At one point, Haas recalls, the two murderers began a lengthy discussion—inviting the prisoners' comments—on the history of art. It is a revealing bit of marginalia. One frequently observes this compulsion in certain Nazis to rub elbows with the esthetic. Goering may have reached for his gun when he heard the word "culture," but it did not prevent him from looting museums and churches all over Europe. Konrad Heiden's "Armed Bohemians" were ruling the world.

The meandering discussion, Haas felt, was not completely off the mark. He sensed that the interrogators were leading to the critical paintings. Such lofty rhetorical queries as "What is the true function of art?" coming from these booted scoundrels may seem ludicrous in retrospect, the stuff of a black comedy, an absurd novel, but it had a certain logic for the SS.

This rather amiable discussion appeared to peter out. At that point, three or four works by each of the artists were produced. There were four Nazi officers present and four artists. (Troller, who was only marginally involved, and Strass, the art buyer, were not included in the interrogation.) Haas' inquisitor was Captain Günther. He was particularly aroused by a depiction of Jews searching a pile of garbage for potato peelings, in Haas' work *Hunger*.

"How could you think up such a mockery of reality, and draw it?" Günther asked. There was a good deal less *bonhomie* in the air by now. Still, Günther seemed to be more curious than angry.

Haas responded in a civil manner, knowing that nothing could be gained by provoking them, that the drawing was not an invention, but the truth. He had, many times, seen people picking at garbage for food. Any painter, Haas argued, is always on the alert for subjects, and he had merely made the sketch while working in the *Zeichenstube* or making his rounds of the camp. It had never occurred to him to mock reality or distort anything. "Do you really think," Günther then asked, "that there is hunger in this ghetto, when the Red Cross could not find any at all?"

Haas does not remember his answer. But now he and the others realized how closely related to the inspection their arrests were.

Slowly, imperceptibly, a new line of interrogation was emerging. What, asked the Germans, were the names of the people outside who had smuggled out this *Greuelpropaganda* and were now distributing it? Were they members of a communist cell? Who were the *apparatchiki?* How many? It seemed to the artists that the Germans surely knew that the pictures had been spirited out by old Strass, who was hardly a revolutionary, but a rather conservative old department-store owner. But they persisted: there had to be a communist plot. All the artists denied the charge. They had painted and sketched for their artistic fulfillment, nothing else.

At Eichmann's order, the questioning was broken off. Fritta, Bloch, Ungar and Haas were ordered to the cellar again. It was a warm, humid day, but they shivered in the underground room. After several hours, Günther and Moes entered. Moes carried a long-barreled pistol. This time there were no philosophical inquiries into the history of art. Their aim was to learn the artists' connection with a communist ring outside the camp. If they revealed the names of the people who had led them into

114

this scurrilous action against the Reich, they would be released. It was apparently inconceivable that a personal sense of outrage could have led the men to paint as they did.

Once again, the men said they could tell the interrogators nothing; there was no communist ring; they had no outside contacts. Moes then threatened them with his leveled pistol; still they would tell him nothing. In disgust, Moes advised Günther, who was ready to start bullying them again, "Stop it! You'll get nothing out of these fellows." They departed. A cold silence descended over the group. No one spoke. Years later, Leo Haas was to write: "We were left alone, and we felt we would never get home again."

By now it had grown dark in the cellar. Outside, they heard the noise of a truck motor, gears grinding in the courtyard. A crowd seemed to be gathering. In a few minutes, a squad of SS men burst into the basement. With gun butts and fists the guards drove the men upstairs and out of the building. Several trucks were waiting for them. In one of them was Strass and his wife, Troller, Bloch's wife, Ungar's wife and their five-year-old daughter, Fritta's wife and their three-year-old son Tomáš, and Haas' wife.

"All of us felt that the worst was about to happen," Troller told me, "but none of us said a word. We remained calm, quiet. Except Ungar. He began to cry. He was a very sensitive man, and a pessimist. His mind kept racing ahead, and he could not control his tears. We would all die, he was certain."

By now it was dusk, and in the humid air a large crowd of silent prisoners gathered to stare at the artists and their families. Among the passers-by was Martha Klein von Peci, the housekeeper for the VIP barracks. She saw the artists and their families huddled together on the trucks and asked one of her "tenants" who was in the crowd what had happened. "They were arrested for having pictures," Baron deHirsch replied. She was terror-stricken. She herself owned a small collection of paintings and sketches. It was nothing to compare with František Strass' store, but if the SS were cracking down on the artists, they might search the entire camp. Over the years, with jars of jam, cigarettes and other delicacies, she had purchased works from Bloch, Jo Spier, and Dr. Fleischmann. At once she hurried to her quarters, where, with the help of another prisoner, she hid some twenty pictures in the paneling of a hollow door. Some of these she still has in her possession, as well as a small book of remembrances of Terezin that includes a water color of her casern by Felix Bloch.

A driver and a guard entered the cab of the first truck. Ungar was still weeping. The others tried to console him. As the engine coughed, they began to speculate.

"One of us said," Troller recalls, "that if the truck turns left, it will mean they are taking us to Prague, and that can't be too bad. But if it turns right, it means the *Kleine Festung*."

The truck turned right.

The *Kleine Festung* was a pile of weathered stones across the river from the main camp. It was said that no Jew ever emerged alive from it.

The group was ordered out of the trucks and told to face the outer wall of the small fort. The detained party now numbered thirteen—the four artists and their wives, Fritta's son, Ungar's daughter, Strass and his wife, and Troller. After several hours of standing, during which time the children cried incessantly, the group was broken up. The men were assigned to one section of the fortress, the women to another, the children to a third.

To appreciate the dismal swamp into which the artists and their families had been plunged we must turn to the eye-witness testimony of Dr. Miloš Bič, a Hussite minister who spent three months in the *Kleine Festung*. Dr. Bič is an expert on Nazi prisons. At various times, this Czech Protestant clergyman was detained in nine jails and work camps, including Dachau and Buchenwald.

"You learn to watch out and dodge blows," Dr. Bič wrote, "but there is one thing you will never understand and that is, how it is possible for man to betray his human dignity as the members of the Gestapo and SS did." Dr. Bič's account continues:

> *Closed in by the walls and mounds of the fortifications, separated from the rest of the world, we were only a little safer when the SS men locked us in our cells. There was nowhere in the camp where we could hide from them, not during work, not during the few hours of free time they sometimes left us on a Sunday afternoon. It was not advisable to meet those who walked through the camp. It was risky to run across to a comrade who lived in different quarters. And it was quite out of the question to speak for, or even do something for, anybody who wore a special mark or was singled out for a special destination. The former were the Jews, noticeable from afar because of the yellow star on their breast and their starved-looking appearance. The latter were those poor souls singled out for extermination whom camp commander Jöckel in fits of sadism let die of starvation in solitary confinement. . . . And we saw others being led to execution, and we heard the reports of the execution squads. . . . The worst treatment was meted out to Jews. They even received orders sometimes to fight one another and were not allowed to stop until one dropped dead. . . . About other brutalities I was told by a man who committed them on the Jews himself. He was a boy of eighteen; his name was John. The SS men appointed him kapo (leader) of the Jews' work group. It was one of his special tasks to kill some Jew every day. He usually chose his victims himself and then he drowned them in the stinking drain passing by the Small Fortress, or he kicked to death those who had been intentionally buried while they were clearing away parts of the walls . . .*

Dr. Bič describes other abominations—SS men forcing prisoners to load wheelbarrows by picking up mouthfuls of dirt;

117

guards using Jews as targets at which they would hurl bricks; endless beatings, humiliations, and when orders came from above—executions.

As nearly as it is possible to reconstruct the events that followed internment in the *Kleine Festung*, it appears that Felix Bloch died a few days after entering the prison, from savage beatings.

František Strass, in his seventies, managed to survive the Little Fortress. Troller remembers him as a snowy-haired, straight-backed aristocrat, with an incredible capacity to absorb punishment. "They would beat him again and again," the architect said, "and he would remain defiant, a hard man to bend." Some months after entering the Little Fortress, Strass and his aged wife were sent to Auschwitz, where both were gassed.

The other men were beaten daily, methodically, with constant demands for information about the communist apparatus that had been disseminating their horror propaganda. Troller, however, was regarded as no direct threat to the Reich, since he was mainly an architect and his drawings were portraits of children. After three months he was released, and sent to Auschwitz.

Bedřich Fritta appears to have aroused the jailers to a frenzy. The man whom Fred Kantor remembers as having "guts" was kicked and pummeled daily, and then contracted a draining case of dysentery. I suspect that Fritta's character was as honest and uncompromising as his bold, truthful drawings. The hand that recorded the ghostly faces of his companions was partner to a soul that could not surrender.

Leo Haas had been separated from the others and was sent to work in a factory in Litoměřice. While working there, he was brutally flogged and developed a serious infection on his leg. In the prison, surgery was performed by two fellow prisoners—a certain Dr. Pavel Wurzel, assisted by a furrier named Julius Taussig. This improbable but competent medical team cured

The Aged Take a Rest by Bedřich Fritta

Haas by cutting away the infected area with a rusty saw! Unable to work, Haas was thrown into an underground cell for incorrigibles. One day Fritta was shoved in to join him. Haas was horrified by his appearance. His friend was like a wraith, shriveled, a wreck of a man ravaged by dysentery. But even in the *Kleine Festung* there were moments of kindness. A Czech prisoner-trusty, a Christian general named Melichar, helped them survive this period through numerous generous acts.

Soon rumors began circulating in the *Kleine Festung*—rumors happily repeated by the "yard commander," a lout named Rojko. Fritta and Haas were to be shot; the Gestapo had decided there was no point in letting them live any longer. These fears were heightened when one day an indictment from the Prague Gestapo office of Captain Hans Günther was read to them.

In it, Fritta and Haas—Ungar had since been shipped to Auschwitz, and Bloch was dead—were charged with perpetrating "horror propaganda" and of "disseminating it abroad." The indictment included, idiotically, a warrant for their arrest, presumably on the assumption that residence in Terezin could not be regarded as internment. Fritta and Haas were ordered to sign the document "for fear of the just anger of the German people." Haas noticed that the paper bore the ominous notation "R.u."—return not desired.

Norbert Troller has told me that he was forced to sign a similar paper just before being sent to Auschwitz. This document, or *Akt*, warned Troller that he could expect "court action against him after the war, in the highest court in Leipzig, for outrageous propaganda against the Reich."

The day after they signed the indictment, Haas and Fritta were herded aboard a freight car bound for Auschwitz. Stops were made at Dresden and Breslau. By now Fritta was barely able to move. Repeated beatings and illness had reduced him to a sack of bones. Every quarter hour, Haas and the other pris-

oners had to carry him to the bucket that served as toilet on the crowded freight car. Dysentery was slowly draining the life from him. When the group disembarked in Dresden for a check at Gestapo headquarters, Haas pleaded with the guards to remove his handcuffs so that he might carry Fritta. They agreed. Fritta was eight years younger than Haas—thirty-five at the time —and a head taller, but the older man managed, bearing him on his back as they stumbled at night through the silent city.

On their arrival at Auschwitz it was apparent that Fritta did not have long to live. He was taken to the infirmary, where the dedicated Dr. Wurzel, who had already saved Haas' life, tried to make him comfortable. But Fritta had crossed some dark and icy frontier; he was beyond rescue. Periodically unconscious, racked by blood poisoning, malnutrition, the cumulative effects of torture, he was scarcely alive. Troller and Haas visited him several times before his death. *"Müde . . . Ich bin müde . . . müde . . ."* he kept mumbling. *Tired . . . I am tired . . . tired . . .*

Other friends visited him. Fritta had always been a gregarious, outgoing man. Food was smuggled in. A scrap of meat would be saved for him; someone would try to cheer him with a funny story. But he had lost the strength to eat, the will to live. In delirium, suffering intractable pain, Bedřich Fritta died eight days after arriving at Auschwitz. This was in August of 1944. The courage and honesty he had put into his drawings had cost him his life.

Leo Haas was more fortunate. Soon after Fritta's death, he was sent to Sachsenhausen. There, because of his artistic talent, he was assigned to a counterfeiting unit, creating the plates for British currency which the Germans planned to use to destroy the pound sterling. The previous team of artists and engravers— all skilled Jewish craftsmen—had been executed. The second group, of which Haas was a member, survived the war. He was liberated in May, 1945, in Ebensee, Austria.

The wives and children of the artists had meanwhile re-mained in the *Kleine Festung*, regarded by the Germans as "small fry of treachery." For more than a year, Haas' wife, Erna, with Hansi Fritta and little Tomáš Fritta, lingered in the notori-ous Fourth Yard of the Little Fortress. A few months after Fritta perished in Auschwitz, Hansi Fritta died of maltreatment and malnutrition in Terezin. Erna Haas, disabled by her long im-prisonment, was still alive when Terezin was liberated in May, 1945. She and her husband adopted Tomáš Fritta, who had en-tered the *Kleine Festung* accompanied by two loving parents, and had emerged an orphan at the age of five. Erna Haas lived for only ten years after being freed, a semi-invalid. Haas re-sumed his career as illustrator, cartoonist, and artist; his sharp, observant pen soon found new modes of expression in films and television.

One of the first things Haas did after the war was to return to Terezin and recover many of the hidden paintings. He located the ones he had secreted in the wall, the tin box with Fritta's works, and many others. Eventually the bulk of these works were donated to the Jewish Museum of Prague.

We must now resume the tragic history of Otto Ungar, who had been sent from Terezin to Auschwitz some time before Fritta and Haas were shipped out. In January of 1945, Ungar participated in one of the worst of the winter death marches, an appalling *Völkerwanderung* from Auschwitz to Buchenwald. That he was alive was in itself miraculous. A gentle, unheroic man, he had been drubbed mercilessly in the *Kleine Festung*. With characteristic savagery, the guards had crushed his right hand to a pulp with their boots and clubs. Two fingers had to be amputated. At some point he had contracted tuberculosis, and possibly typhus.

On January 18, 1945, the SS command in Berlin ordered a

general evacuation of Auschwitz. Russian guns thundered in the distance; the Germans were busy burning records, making excuses. As the wind howled across the plains of Poland and snow swirled about their bare heads, sixty-four thousand prisoners, many of them wearing only their prison pajamas, were sent out to wander across the white hell of Europe. Thousands died of exposure, exhaustion and starvation in the first few days of the march. In this mass of shuffling, moaning humanity, an endless troop of bent figures plodding to one more awful destination across the wind-whipped fields, was Otto Ungar. Incredibly, he lived through the dreadful time, arriving at Buchenwald with fourteen thousand other ghosts of Auschwitz, witnesses to the eerie twilight of the Third Reich.

The new arrivals were shoved into Buchenwald's "Little Camp," a place already permeated with the miasma of death, a hole where no one was expected to live. Spotted typhus broke out. In the last three months of Buchenwald's existence thirteen thousand died. The majority of the prisoners had been reduced to *Mussulmen*, concentration-camp slang for the walking dead, mindless skeletons, stumbling about in a scrap of blanket.

George Straka, a teacher at Strasbourg University, described the arrival of these prisoners—one of whom was Ungar:

Sometimes under pressure of blows they would break suddenly into movement like a herd of cattle, jostling each other. It was impossible to extract from their lips their names, much less the date of their birth. Kindness itself had not the power to make them speak. They would only look at you with a long expressionless stare. If they tried to answer, their tongues could not reach their dried-up palates to make a sound. One was aware only of a poisonous breath appearing to come from entrails already in a state of decomposition. That was what the transports were like in the winter of 1944–45, that winter when death achieved the prodigious figure of thirteen thousand detainees in the last three months before liberation.

Ungar lived out the last months of his life in Buchenwald, a dying man surrounded by corpses and near-corpses. It was at this time that he was observed clutching a piece of coal in his mutilated hand, scratching away at a sheet of paper, still trying to depict the murky inferno into which he and millions of others had been plunged, still trying to force the truth upon a disbelieving world.

The Germans had destroyed his hand, beaten him and starved him; deprived him of the love of his wife and daughter; and finally they took his life. But they could not, and I make no apologies for the lofty expression, destroy his will to create. I think we may be reasonably sure of one thing regarding Ungar's last days. He was no *Mussulman* in those final weeks of agony. They drifted unhearing, unseeing, their grasp on life broken. But not Ungar. A frail man he may have been; a man prone to weep; a worrier and pessimist. But he was still trying to draw. I wish someone had preserved that scrap of paper with its ragged scrawls.

He died on July 25, 1945, almost exactly a year after the day he had been questioned in the SS office in Terezin by Eichmann, Rahm, Günther and Moes. His wife and daughter lived through the holocaust. Troops of the Soviet Army freed them from the Little Fortress in May, 1945.

The Transport Leaving by Bedřich Fritta

Waiting for the Transport to Auschwitz by Bedřich Fritta

Religious Services by Leo Haas

3

There were other artists at Terezin, who did not figure in the "incident" but who contributed to the cultural life of the camp, and played important roles in recording the truth about it.

One whom I have already mentioned was Dr. Karel Fleischmann. He was never a member of the group that worked in the *Zeichenstube*. A physician—specifically a dermatologist—he was attached to the Terezin hospital. Fleischmann was born in 1897 in Klatovy, Bohemia, the son of a typographer, attended secondary and medical schools in Bohemia, and practiced medicine in České Budějovice. But a successful practice, expertise with rashes and inflammations, were not enough to satisfy his intellectual curiosity. He was also a skilled artist, and published collections of woodcuts and lithographs. Occasionally he wrote short stories and poems.

In April, 1942, Dr. Fleischmann and his wife were arrested and sent to Terezin. There he joined the brave company of ghetto doctors who struggled daily against filth, hunger, overcrowding and a shortage of medicine. Fleischmann had a sense of humor, a talent for laughter. He was a man who naturally eased the discomfort of others, who transmitted his own capacity for joy and wonder.

This quality is reflected in his works. *The Torah Reading on the Sabbath* is revealing. Despite the strained faces of the elders of the congregation, there is inspiration, courage in them—the same courage Dr. Fleischmann displayed during his medical rounds. *Theater Performance* is another notable work—the high walls of the barracks rising above the tiny stage and the massed audience fail to diminish the enthusiasm, the vitality of performers and onlookers. But he was not an artist to blind himself to the cruel truths of Terezin. The already mentioned *First Night of New Arrivals* and the chilling *Mortuary* speak to us in the same tortured tones that Fritta and Haas employed.

In one account of Terezin I came across a reference to Dr. Fleischmann in which he was described as "an enthusiastic dilettante." During one of my interviews, I used these words. The woman to whom I was speaking, who had known Dr. Fleischmann, was indignant. "He was no dilettante," she said firmly; "he was a marvelous man, and good at everything he did, as a doctor, an artist, a writer."

I'm certain he was. There is something mistily saddening about Fleischmann. Doctors have always seemed to me—the best of them at any rate—touched with some special knowledge. Perhaps more than the religious, they are intermediaries for us, interposing themselves between us and darkness. They imbue their calling with small litanies, rituals, cunningly conceived to defeat pain, to cheat death. The touch of two fingers on a pulsating wrist; a quiet voice assuring us, *Just lie still a minute, it won't hurt*; a scrawl on a prescription pad. Credit it to hypochondria or to having been raised in a doctor's house—I cherish these prejudices.

In my mind's eye I see Dr. Fleischmann, probably a man of modest stature in a dark, rumpled suit, a battered Homburg on his head (did he wear horn-rimmed glasses?), carrying a scuffed black bag as he makes his rounds in the model ghetto. I am sure

A Street in Terezin by Hugo Sonnenschein

Small Town by Ruth Schacterova

Man's Silhouette in the Mountains by unknown child

Theater Performance by Sona Spitzova

The Torah Reading on the Sabbath by Karel Fleischmann

Mortuary by Karel Fleischmann

he was kept very busy. They died at the rate of 130 a day. The physicians of Terezin never suffered from a lack of patients.

There is one relevant detail about his appearance. He was slightly deformed—one shoulder being lower than the other. It was a minor disability, and did not in any way hamper his medical work or the zest he brought to his painting and writing. Twenty-five years after his death, he remains, to my mind, a paradigm of those talented, compassionate professional men whom the Jews of Central Europe produced in such astonishing number and variety, and who by dint of their very humaneness, their accomplishments, had to be obliterated by the Nazis. Dr. Fleischmann, as I see him, was a *Mensch*.

In October, 1944, the physician and his wife were ordered to Auschwitz. It proved to be one of the last shipments from Terezin. Only a few weeks prior, the deceitful stratagem of the "family camps" had been perpetrated. Records show that the last Terezin transport arrived at Birkenau-Auschwitz on October 30. It is possible that the Fleischmanns were members of it. To the end, I am certain, he was bandaging wounds, taking pulses, dispensing aspirin.

Dr. Norbert Frŷd, a Czech diplomat and writer, was a close friend of Karel Fleischmann. They were from the same town in Bohemia. Frŷd was at Auschwitz with him. The two men stood a few paces apart at the moment of selection. At the head of the line was an SS officer, making the choices. At the last moment, Frŷd remembers, the German noticed Dr. Fleischmann's deformed shoulder, and deemed him unworthy to live. The doctor and his wife were assigned to the gas chambers.

Petr Kien was only twenty-two when he arrived at Terezin in 1941. Kien was from Varnsdorf in the Sudetenland, where his father had owned a small textile factory. After the Munich Pact,

Self-Portrait by Petr Kien

when Germany took over the region, Kien moved to Prague. He studied art, and for a while, like Bedřich Fritta, whom he knew, he conducted art classes. Kien was a student of the well-known Czech artist Willi Nowak, an outspokenly anti-Nazi figure, who influenced the young pupil. Kien, like Fleischmann, was good at many things. He was a graphic artist, a caricaturist, and was a poet and writer. Both of his parents were at Terezin. In 1944, they were sent to Auschwitz, and Petr joined them voluntarily. All three were killed there.

A remarkable self-portrait by Petr Klein, made when he was only seventeen years of age, survives. The artist portrays himself as a slender, gawky youth with oversized hands and wrists depending from an ill-fitting gray suit. The features are large; there is a wondering expression on the youthful face. The outraged eyes are the disbelieving eyes of every young adult in the world, every young man recently graduated from childhood into a grown-up world that he does not quite trust. Who could blame the seventeen-year-old Petr Kien? It is a prophetic, achingly truthful picture. I studied it for a long time, for it seemed I had known so many Petr Kiens, the knowing young, with their offended eyes. The longer I looked at it, the longer I sensed some literary association, some unaware rendering of a fictional figure. Was it Kafka's K.? Or young Werther? Suddenly I knew. Kien had painted a Central European Holden Caulfield.

There were many other artists who pursued their work in Terezin—the impressionist Mme. Argitinska; the sculptor Zadikov; Professor Stein, a dignified old man "who looked like Rachmaninoff"; Malvína Schálková; Adolf Aussenberg; and Fred Kantor, who kept a revealing sketchbook of daily life.

Terezin also produced the famous children's pictures. In 1942, Dr. Fleischmann wrote: "One of us will teach these chil-

135

Women at Work by Malvína Schálková

Women's Dwellings by Malvína Schálková

dren how to sing again, to write on paper with a pencil, to do sums and multiply. One of us is sure to survive."

Nazi thoroughness saw to it that very few of the children survived to fulfill Dr. Fleischmann's hope. Of more than fifteen thousand interned at Terezin, about 150 lived. For most of them, the end of the road was Auschwitz. Nor did the kind physician live to teach a child to paint, spell or do sums, when the nightmare was ended.

Doch einen Schmetterling hab Ich nicht hier gesehen. . . . But I haven't seen a butterfly here. The Terezin poem by a young boy named Pavel is of a piece with the children's touching paintings. In their hopeful minds they saw butterflies, and flowers, and the joyful life they had left behind; and they painted these, and wrote about them.

Children's life in the ghetto, for the most part, was a collective existence. A handful of youngsters lived with their parents. But the majority of them were housed in huge collective barracks, two hundred or three hundred to a building, about twenty to forty to a room. Actually, it was an effective way of making the youngsters more comfortable, assuring better food distribution, medical care. The decision was that of the *Judenältester*. The Germans had no particular interest in the children, and let the Jewish officials handle them as they saw fit. As in many instances in the camps, organization made life more bearable.

Although conditions for education were extremely unfavorable, a school system was organized at once. Classes were held in the same rooms where the children slept and ate. There was a severe shortage of books, and the transient nature of camp population made it difficult to preserve any continuity of classes and teachers. But almost all children up to fifteen years of age received some kind of schooling.

Some parents refused to put their children in the school— not for any anti-intellectual bias, but for more practical reasons.

One woman to whom I spoke, the widow of a leader of the Prague Jewish community who had been shot early during the occupation, explained to me why she would not let her twelve-year-old son attend the classes. "I had my choice for Josef—school or work on the farm," she said. "I chose the farm. He would have fresh air, exercise, more food. There would be plenty of time to educate him, if we lived to be liberated." Mrs. Ruckmann proved to be a good prophet. Outdoor work kept Josef in good health. He and his mother were among the lucky survivors, and he was indeed educated later on.

It of course does not follow that a refusal to attend school or seek the intellectual life in the camps ensured survival. But there is a connection. Indeed, it raises the entire question of the value of Terezin's elaborate cultural life—the concerts, lectures, art exhibitions and library. It is a complex question, and I raise it because it runs throughout many concentration-camp experiences.

Put bluntly, the Nazis did prefer to murder scholars rather than laborers. Laborers had a utilitarian value; scholars were superfluous. I shall cite a perfect example. A former Terezin inmate—I'll call him Dr. Kohn—had been a well-known linguist in Prague. He had taught German, French and Hebrew at the high-school level. He went off to Terezin as a young man, burly, powerful, easygoing. "When I was in the reception center in the Prague Fair," he told me, "a man next to me said, 'Kohn, take your eyeglasses off and stick them in your pocket. The Germans hate anyone wearing horn-rimmed glasses. It means you are educated, an intellectual, and they'll make it hard for you.'"

Once inside the camp, Dr. Kohn was given his choice of jobs by the *Judenältester*. They wanted him to teach, but they would not insist on it. Like Mrs. Ruckmann where her son was concerned, Dr. Kohn felt he would serve himself better by working on the farm. And so he did—digging, planting, harvesting, out of

Distribution of Bread by Karel Fleischmann

Night Funeral by Otto Ungar

doors most of the time. His limbs grew hard, his hands callused.

Later, Dr. Kohn had an even stranger decision to make. Under Eichmann's prodding, one of those lunatic "research" projects into Jewish history was to be undertaken at Terezin. (Eichmann, another dabbler, always passed himself off as an "expert" in Jewish history and the Talmud.) This study group, to be known as the *Talmud Hundertschaft*, was to comprise Jewish scholars, linguists and biblical experts. They would be charged with producing a new authoritative translation of the Talmud into German. One can only speculate dazedly on the meanderings of the German mind; in the midst of murdering every Jew in Europe, they still presented themselves with a patina of scholarship. Once more we see the Armed Bohemians in control.

"Don't volunteer for the *Talmud Hundertschaft*," old Professor Stein warned Dr. Kohn. "Whenever the Nazis set up one of these study teams, they send them all to the East when it's over or when they get tired of it. Work on the farm."

Dr. Kohn took this advice. Summoned to the SS command—Eichmann was present, as he always seemed to be when cultural matters were raised—Dr. Kohn stumbled through his audition. He read his Hebrew poorly and denied that he had any special expertise in the language, other than having studied it for his bar mitzvah. The Germans were vaguely suspicious, but they excused him. Professor Stein was proved correct. Most of the scholars in the *Talmud Hundertschaft* were exterminated. Dr. Kohn, suppressing his intellectual gifts, eyeglasses in pocket, chose the hoe over the pen, and lived.

Of course disavowal of intellect did not necessarily mean survival. Mrs. Ruckmann's son and Dr. Kohn did not necessarily survive because they labored in the fields. And the schoolchildren and Talmudists did not necessarily die because they read books and painted butterflies and translated old texts. But cause-

and-effect was at work, perhaps best viewed through Dr. Kohn's comment: "The Germans hated anyone wearing horn-rimmed glasses."

Yet I wonder what choice the Terezin Jews had, especially where their fifteen thousand children were concerned. Ideally, if we were to follow Bruno Bettelheim's advice, the children should have been organized in commandos, taught karate and knife-fighting, formed resistance cells, sabotaged the Germans' industries, and when the time came for transport, died tearing at the throats of the SS guards.

What are we to make of these Czech Jews—spending long hours in makeshift classrooms, sketching Passover seders of a world that had vanished, arranging musical evenings, rehearsing *The Bartered Bride*, dutifully attending lectures on Plato, teaching their doomed children to do sums and read, acting as if Terezin were a cultural haven, and blinding themselves to the fires? I'm not sure I know. The vast majority of them eventually were killed, including all the artists except Leo Haas. Would they have been better off dying a year, a month, a week sooner, in some bold, defiant act, garroting Captain Rahm or knifing Haindl? We know that Terezin was loosely guarded. But we can also imagine how the relatively bearable life of the camp would have changed—witness the all-day census—had there been even a single act of rebellion.

Would an act of mass revolt have served any purpose or did it offer any encouragement at all to the prisoners? Suppose the *Aufbaukommando*, back in December of 1941, gathered in the Terezin town square, getting their orders from two— *two!*—SS men, decided to jump them, kill them, and flee? Where would they go? Was there any guarantee that the Czechs would open their hearts to them—342 wanted men? Let us remember that this was 1941. No one knew of any Final Solution; no one knew about the gas chambers. Moreover, the *Aufbaukom-*

mando was largely a volunteer unit. Bedřich Fritta and the others had gone willingly to the model ghetto.

I'm afraid it's too easy for us, safe, secure, years removed from the tragedy, to shake our heads, roll our eyes, and pronounce: *They should have fought back*. What would I have done in 1941, aged nineteen, young, strong, eager to live, full of plans? I think I would have done just what the *Aufbaukommando* men did. It would never have occurred to me that I was cooperating in an intricate scheme to murder all my people. The comfort I can draw from the critics, however, is that they post a warning: *Never again*. I have the feeling that most Jews have learned the lesson.

Another point. We surely do not need the tiresome "wisdom" of Chairman Mao to explain to us that the people are the water and the guerrillas are the fish. In much of Nazi-occupied Europe, particularly the East, had more Jews been daring enough to play the fish, I am afraid they would have found the waters swarming with hungry sharks. Even at this late date, when sometimes it is prudent to let bygones be bygones, one is filled with a wasting nausea at reading about the dutiful manner in which Polish and Ukrainian resistance fighters—themselves hunted by the Germans!—found the time and energy to murder Jewish escapees or partisans who turned to them and tried to make common cause. Every intelligent, sensitive Pole I have ever met cringes and grows uneasy when you say to him *Warsaw Ghetto*. He knows, he knows. And he is terribly sorry. Some of us acted a bit better, you understand . . . not all of us . . .

I wonder sometimes how people manage to live down a national disgrace. The ghetto fought the Germans; and the Poles rested on their guns, and smiled—let the Nazis get on with their killings. The SS men also smiled. (Study the photographs of the final roundup of the ghetto people—the beaten women and children with hands raised, German soldiers smirking.) I find it hard to weep when I read about the cynical manner in which the Red Army, in turn, stacked rifles and permitted the Nazis to destroy the Polish resistance in Warsaw a few years later.

Maybe the Jews could not have fought too well, the critic can still argue, but more of them could have run away. I wonder. A Czech woman I spoke to told me that four of her brothers had fled from Prague to the Soviet Union when the Germans occupied the city. She herself was in Terezin, then Auschwitz, and while on one of those horrendous winter marches, escaped, and hid in farmhouses in Silesia. Wandering east, she came upon a Red Army unit. The officers, learning she was a Czech, told her that a Czech brigade was several miles to the rear. She hurried there in search of her brothers, since she knew that the majority of the soldiers in the brigade were Czech Jews. She found *one* brother. The other three had been executed by the Russians as spies. "*Spion*," she told me—and began to weep. I looked at the photos of the four brothers, the pretty sister—kids on a Prague street, fat, well-dressed Jewish kids. Europe had plans for them.

Surely Terezin was the classic example of the "business as usual" attitude which, some argue, helped speed the destruction of the Jews. In many ways, Terezin, that sham, that *Paradeisghetto*, where Jews were cajoled, fed on false promises, used to deceive the world, may well be one of the most disturbing cases of nonresistance. But I am not certain.

What, we may ask, was the proper mode of behavior for a Terezin prisoner? Dr. H. G. Adler, a German psychologist, who was interned there, tried to formulate an answer to the question. How can Judaism thrive in slavery while awaiting death in the camps? He is said to have grown bleakly pessimistic, that none of the answers satisfied him. Adler found only one man who, he felt, had shown an authentic Jewish response. This was Leo Baeck, the elderly Chief Rabbi of Berlin, one of the privileged prisoners. Daily, Adler observed the old rabbi taking care of the

Portraits by Karel Fleischmann

elderly and ill, lecturing on Plato and Kant, helping to pull garbage wagons, devoting time to the children's care services. The Germans had expected him to die in Terezin, but were reluctant to kill him. He might someday prove a useful hostage. An incredible dialogue between Rabbi Baeck and Eichmann once occurred, revealing the Germans' ambivalent feelings about the old man. "Herr Baeck," the chief of the Gestapo's Jewish Section exclaimed, "are you still alive? I thought you were dead!" The rabbi responded, "You are apparently announcing a future occurrence." Later, Eichmann consulted his files and found an erroneous entry of Baeck's death. "I understand now," Eichmann commented cheerfully, no doubt pleased by his wit: "a man who gets himself entered as dead lives longer!"

Rabbi Baeck's case is worth study, if we are to pursue the Bettelheim thesis, as well as Dr. Adler's speculations on proper behavior. It was this same Baeck, whom Dr. Adler regarded as the paradigm of moral Judaism, *who kept the truth of Auschwitz from his fellow prisoners!* As early as 1941, Baeck had information from Poland about certain buses that were equipped with gassing devices. He told no one. In 1943 a Czech engineer named Grünberg, who had sneaked into Terezin to impart the news, told Baeck a more detailed story of the gas chambers. "Everyone at Auschwitz knows it," Grünberg said. But Rabbi Baeck relayed not a word to the *Judenältester* or, as far as is known, to anyone else. "Living in expectation of death by gassing would only be harder," he wrote later. There was always the chance that some might live, that extermination was not inevitable for all.

How are we to judge Dr. Baeck's silence? If Dr. Adler regarded him as the exemplar of noble behavior in the camp, how does he stack up in terms of Bettelheim's standards? Rather poorly, I would say. He was a "business as usual" Jew, keeping the truth from people who might have rebelled.

But when all the evidence is sorted, I find it very hard to condemn Dr. Baeck or the harassed *Judenältester* or the artists who labored in the *Zeichenstube*. I find no historic parallels for the thorough and devious manner in which the Germans applied themselves to their task. I find nothing in the Jewish *Zeitgeist* to make for an aroused, armed struggle. I find it hard to be critical of the victims. Again, I keep coming back to the behavior of Germans, Poles, Lithuanians—and, yes, Americans—during these frightful years. Just as I believe that an examination of the attitudes of white America is more relevant if we hope to cure our racial sickness than endless analyses of black power, black motivation, black words, needs and deeds.

What judgment is to be made on Ungar, clutching his lump of coal in Buchenwald? Or Fritta, beaten to a bloody pulp, ravaged by disease, dying in Auschwitz, too tired to live? Or Peter Kien, that eternal teen-ager, studying the deceiving adult world with the horrified eyes of a Czech Holden Caulfield? Or Dr. Fleischmann, the good physician, standing at the edge of the gassing rooms, betrayed by a sloping shoulder? How shall we judge their activities in Terezin, and by extension, the co-operative game played by most of its Jews?

It is tempting to state that they were too complaisant, that they had no right to accept their privileged jobs, where they could sit day after day turning out organizational charts. Hindsight affords us a tawdry moral stance; I find it hard to assume it. If the artists were wrong to cooperate, what about the *Judenältester* who made the selections for transport, or the managers and directors who staged *Carmen* and *The Bartered Bride*, or the lecturers who spoke of Kant, or the teachers who worked with the children—indeed, all those engaged in the cultural efforts that in large measure sustained the notion that Terezin was a little village of happy Jews?

Deluded they may have been, misled by false optimism. Per-

149

Sketches by Bedřich Fritta

haps a few even harbored that secret death wish of which Dr. Bettelheim has written. Perhaps it might be argued that by pursuing this parody of their real lives within the walls of Terezin, they kept the inmates hopeful, distracted, and helped grease the rails to Auschwitz. Unquestionably it suited Eichmann and his gang to continue this charade. It made for good propaganda; the Red Cross would be delighted. But I suspect that the Jews of Terezin did what they did *naturally*. What was more natural than a library, concerts, schools, lectures, and exhibitions of paintings?

Like the juggler who performed for the Virgin, the artists made their protest as best they knew how. Fritta's potent sketches, speaking of fear and desolation; Haas' merciless caricatures of his jailers; Ungar's sensitive evocation of ordinary people; Fleischmann's compassionate images of men trying to preserve sanity and decency in hell—all these works seem to me to be protests, moral statements of the noblest order. Surely the Germans regarded the smuggled, secret works as a threat to them. *Greuelpropaganda!* they screamed. Eichmann denounced the artists as ingrates and liars. I have the suspicion that it may have taken as much courage to draw these grim scenes of the mortuary, the attic, the soup kitchen, and the executions as it would have to strangle Sergeant Schultz.

I am encouraged enormously by the survival of the Terezin pictures and the attention they have received. Those ghosts crammed into Fritta's attic, Fleischmann's sorrowing "New Arrivals," the dehumanized wrecks standing around the soup barrels shiver us with hard truths, with the inescapable tragedies of our time.

"Depend upon it, sir," said Dr. Johnson, "when a man is to be hanged in a fortnight, it concentrates his mind wonderfully."

152

In the context of the Terezin artists, I do not think the comment frivolous or cruel. What I find so engrossing in their work is subject matter, style, conviction. These works are true acts of resistance, of defiance, of artists working with brain and heart to tear down Nazi lies, to outstare the jailer, to condemn the virulence and fraud of the Third Reich.

In a sense the Germans were correct when they denounced the works as horror propaganda. And perhaps the finest tribute ever paid to the artists was the plaintive query of Major Hans Günther, Eichmann's "referent" in Prague, when he asked Leo Haas:

"How could you think up such a mockery of reality, and draw it?"

I suspect that Haas treasured that question as much as he did comments by friendly critics.

Old Age Home by Otto Ungar

4

This account of the Terezin artists concludes with some notes on the last days of the camp, even though the men about whom I have written were not directly concerned with that strange surrealist period. But how I wish they *had* been on hand to witness the decay of Nazi power, the final dotty pirouettes of the *Übermenschen*! It was a time that cried for Fritta's stark pen, for Fleischmann's compassionate eye, Haas' devastating hand.

The Reich crumbled. The filth under the flesh was revealed, the corruption and loathsomeness visible to all. Beneath that courageous blond Nordic mask, that pure white skin, there was no muscle or blood or bone, just worms, garbage, pus and offal. Prophetic Trotsky! He had looked at German National Socialism in the early thirties, and said, "Everything which society, if it had developed normally, would have rejected as the excrement of culture, is now bursting through its throat."

And still the Germans lied, wheedled, bargained, worked their transparent deceits. One would be moved to hoot and whistle, were it not all so appallingly shameless. In the fading hours of Hitler's Third Reich, we discover Heinrich Himmler, the archetypical middle-class man, unsuccessful chicken farmer, a wheyfaced fellow, pince-nez perched on snub nose, trying to use Terezin as his "passport to respectability," in Gerald Reitlinger's apt phrase. Here was the Nazi spirit at its most refined—crafty, selfish, acting with that blameless innocence, that sense of "we're both civilized men, let's talk this over." If Goebbels and Hitler were the "Armed Bohemians" of Nazidom, then Himmler was its "Armed Bourgeois."

On April 5, 1945, one month before *Götterdämmerung*, with the walls collapsing, with the Red Army thundering across Czechoslovakia, the tireless Eichmann, another reasonable fellow, showed up at Terezin. He was there at Himmler's orders and he had with him M. Paul Dunant of the Swiss Red Cross, whom he personally escorted around the *Paradeisghetto* to show him how decently the Jews had been handled. The Germans were still convinced that Terezin could cancel out a multitude of sins, and they tested its efficacy to the very last. This paranoid's gavotte, Eichmann and the Red Cross man waltzing in and out of the Terezin barracks with much bowing and explaining and conversation, is stupefying. "It was a very formal occasion," Gerald Reitlinger wrote, "and in the evening Lieutenant General Karl Frank, Protector for Bohemia and Moravia, gave the delegation a reception in the Hradschin Palace in Prague."

The reception was an elaborate affair, under crystal chandeliers, tables sparkling with silver and creamy linen. The visitors merited such treatment, for they had spent a tiring day on the Terezin tour. Buildings had again been scrubbed, the dead and dying shoved out of sight, Red Cross parcels distributed. Josef Polak's history of Terezin wryly records that M. Dunant left Terezin "greatly satisfied." At the reception that evening, Eichmann worked his magic on him with great fervor, with pathetic sincerity.

Not enough has been written about these leisure-time activities of the Nazis. Anyone fascinated, as I am, with the abysmal brute should read Curzio Malaparte's pitiless account of European Fascism from the inside, *Kaputt*. Malaparte may have lied when it suited him, but no one can doubt the accuracy of the banquets and balls he describes—festivities on top of the bone-yard. There is Hans Frank, charming, laughing, champagne guzzling, full of witty stories, pensive as the pianist performs Chopin, flattering the bare-shouldered women in gowns—and several hundred yards away the SS takes target practice on Jewish children trying to sneak out of the ghetto. (Maybe people like Malaparte have told us more than we should know. They tend to discourage even limited optimists.)

How I wish Fritta or Haas had been able to hide behind an arras, sketch pad in hand, to immortalize in a few strokes that last meeting at Hradschin Palace! Eichmann, his eyes gleaming, crowded M. Dunant into a corner of the great salon. Amid the baroque splendor, the ormolu frames and sparkling crystal, he informed the Swiss inspector that all that Herr Himmler had ever wanted was for "the Jews to acquire a sense of racial community through the exercise of almost complete autonomy." M. Dunant's response is not known. Could he have asked about the gassings? Probably not. We can envision them promenading around the ballroom, sipping slivovitz and cognac after a dinner of roast goose and dumplings. Eichmann was in an expansive mood—philosophic, thoughtful. Really, he told Dunant, the Jews in Terezin were better off than many Germans. The scratched old record played on.

Dunant inquired: what would happen to the Jews *after* they had acquired this treasured sense of autonomy in places like Terezin? That had been planned for, the chief of the Jewish Section replied. Jews would be transported to "some region" where they could live separate from the German population. It was as simple as that. Himmler had thought it all out. Eichmann became confidential. He personally did not approve of all those humane measures that Himmler was going to introduce vis-à-vis the Jews, but Eichmann, "good soldier that he was," would obey them.

Other moments in Terezin's last hours deserved a Fritta or a Fleischmann. Ten days after M. Dunant's "inspection" with Eichmann, a convoy of Swedish buses, accompanied by Swedish guides in white uniforms, arrived to evacuate the camp's 423 Danish Jews. An incident occurred that symbolized the end of the rule of King Toad, an omen that the sleep of reason was over. Captain Hans Günther looked on glumly as the Danish Jews boarded the vehicles. Rahm and Haindl stood at his side. Suddenly Haindl, all bluff cheeriness, made to board one of the Swedish buses. An image worthy of Haas comes to mind—the cigar-chomping assistant commandant, in pressed black uniform, smiling to his fellow northerner, one booted foot on the running board. We understand one another, *nicht wahr?* But the Swedish driver barred his way. "You are on international territory," he told Haindl; "you cannot come aboard."

Change was in the wind. Small rebuke for mass murderers, but the Jews were in no position to bargain for more. Two days later Rahm assembled the twenty thousand people who remained in Terezin, stiffened his back and addressed them as *"Meine Herren!"* The nightmare was almost over.

But not entirely. An influx of Jews from Poland touched off a devastating typhus epidemic. The Red Cross flag was raised over the camp; the SS detachment and Commandant Rahm fled. The first American to enter the liberated camp was the journalist and novelist Meyer Levin. In his memorable book *In Search*, Levin wrote:

> *We emerged into the courtyard, and just then a wagon drove through the archway: it carried the daily ration of bread. A husky young woman stood on the wagon to carry out the distribution but*

she was helpless. The vehicle was instantly mobbed, and from all corners the mob increased; we were caught in it as the ravenous survivors, oblivious of the shrieks of women trampled upon, or of cries from the camp police for order, unheeding to any appeal or command, raged and tore at each other to reach the wagon.

On May 11, 1945, advance units of the Soviet Army arrived. A medical team was established at Terezin, and the epidemic was arrested. The great Potemkin Village, the Habsburg fortress that nobody had even bothered to take, was again metamorphosing. The Jews departed—back to Czech cities and towns, to Holland, Hungary, Yugoslavia, Romania, and to the beckoning Middle East, to Zion. Incredibly, within a few days after liberation the original Christian residents of Terezin began to drift back—as if nothing, nothing at all, had occurred in four years.

Fritta, Bloch, Dr. Fleischmann, Kien, were all dead. Leo Haas was alive, liberated in Ebensee. Ungar lay dying in a hospital near Weimar.

"Hath not a Jew hands?" the merchant asked. He not only has them, but they are often—like Ungar's—crushed and broken to destroy their power to create. Indeed, the hands of Jews are known to have had nails driven through them.

I keep thinking about the artists' hand. At night, in the barracks, in the drafting studio, they gave the lie to the model ghetto, defied the murderer, and performed what is, after all, the noblest function of art—to assist blundering mankind in its pained search for bits and pieces of truth.

When Conrad wrote that the artist "speaks to our capacity for delight and wonder, to the sense of mystery surrounding our lives; to our sense of pity, and beauty and pain," he might have been writing about the artists of Terezin. *Pity, beauty and pain.* The triad is present in full measure in Fritta's spectral workers,

159

in Haas' aged, in Fleischmann's readers of the Torah, in Ungar's heroic panorama of Terezin with its stooped residents shuffling through bleak streets beneath a darkling sky.

"We are healed of suffering only by experiencing it to the full," Proust observed. Perhaps these truthful and courageous pictures are part of that long, painful process of healing. We can at least hope so.

Poems and Drawings
by the
Children of Terezin

YES, THAT'S THE WAY THINGS ARE

I.

In Terezin in the so-called park
A queer old granddad sits
Somewhere there in the so-called park.
He wears a beard down to his lap
And on his head, a little cap.

II.

Hard crusts he crumbles in his gums,
He's only got one single tooth.
My poor old man with working gums,
Instead of soft rolls, lentil soup.
My poor old grey-beard!

Koleba (M. Košek, H. Löwy, Bachner)

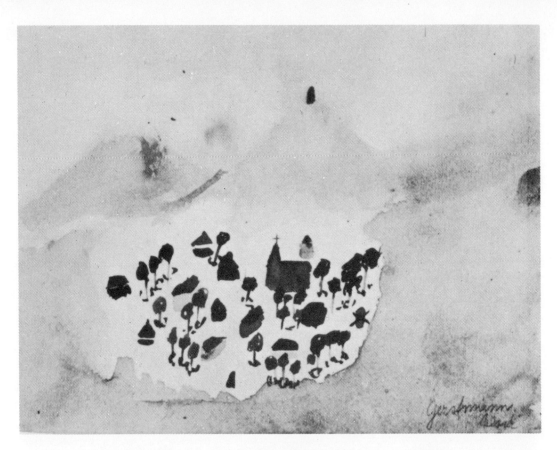

AT TEREZIN

When a new child comes
Everything seems strange to him.
What, on the ground I have to lie?
Eat black potatoes? No! Not I!
I've got to stay? It's dirty here!
The floor—why, look, it's dirt, I fear!
And I'm supposed to sleep on it?
I'll get all dirty!

Here the sound of shouting, cries,
And oh, so many flies.
Everyone knows flies carry disease.
Oooh, something bit me! Wasn't that a bedbug?
Here in Terezin, life is hell
And when I'll go home again, I can't yet tell.

"Teddy"

169

FEAR

Today the ghetto knows a different fear,
Close in its grip, Death wields an icy scythe.
An evil sickness spreads a terror in its wake,
The victims of its shadow weep and writhe.

Today a father's heartbeat tells his fright
And mothers bend their heads into their hands.
Now children choke and die with typhus here,
A bitter tax is taken from their bands.

My heart still beats inside my breast
While friends depart for other worlds.
Perhaps it's better—who can say?—
Than watching this, to die today?

No, no, my God, we want to live!
Not watch our numbers melt away.
We want to have a better world,
We want to work—we must not die!

Eva Picková, 12 years old, Nymburk

172

THE BUTTERFLY

The last, the very last,
So richly, brightly, dazzlingly yellow.
    Perhaps if the sun's tears would sing
    against a white stone . . .

Such, such a yellow
Is carried lightly 'way up high.
It went away I'm sure because it wished to
    kiss the world goodbye.

For seven weeks I've lived in here,
Penned up inside this ghetto
But I have found my people here.
The dandelions call to me
And the white chestnut candles in the court.
Only I never saw another butterfly.

That butterfly was the last one.
Butterflies don't live in here,
    In the ghetto.

Pavel Friedmann

IT ALL DEPENDS ON HOW YOU LOOK AT IT

I.

Terezin is full of beauty.
It's in your eyes now clear
And through the street the tramp
Of many marching feet I hear.

In the ghetto at Terezin,
It looks that way to me,
Is a square kilometer of earth
Cut off from the world that's free.

II.

Death, after all, claims everyone,
You find it everywhere.
It catches up with even those
Who wear their noses in the air.

The whole, wide world is ruled
With a certain justice, so
That helps perhaps to sweeten
The poor man's pain and woe.

Miroslav Košek

181

POHŘEB

TEREZIN

The heaviest wheel rolls across our foreheads
To bury itself deep somewhere inside our memories.

We've suffered here more than enough,
Here in this clot of grief and shame,
Wanting a badge of blindness
To be a proof for their own children.

A fourth year of waiting, like standing above a swamp
From which any moment might gush forth a spring.

Meanwhile, the rivers flow another way,
Another way,
Not letting you die, not letting you live.

And the cannons don't scream and the guns don't bark
And you don't see blood here.
Nothing, only silent hunger.
Children steal the bread here and ask and ask
                    and ask
And all would wish to sleep, keep silent and
          just to go to sleep again . . .

The heaviest wheel rolls across our foreheads
To bury itself deep somewhere inside our memories.

THE GARDEN

A little garden,
Fragrant and full of roses.
The path is narrow
And a little boy walks along it.

A little boy, a sweet boy,
Like that growing blossom.
When the blossom comes to bloom,
The little boy will be no more.

Franta Bass

I'D LIKE TO GO ALONE

I'd like to go away alone
Where there are other, nicer people,
Somewhere into the far unknown,
There, where no one kills another.

Maybe more of us,
A thousand strong,
Will reach this goal
Before too long.

Alena Synková

Chronology

1939 *March 5*	German Army enters Prague. German Protectorate of Bohemia and Moravia established.
July 26	Central Bureau for the Relocation of Jews set up. Census of Czech Jewish population begun.
December 1	Jewish children excluded from state schools.
1940 *June 14*	Auschwitz concentration camp set up.
1941 *September 27*	Reinhard Heydrich named acting Reichsprotector; soon orders the deportation of Jews and the establishment of Terezin as a Jewish ghetto.
October 16	First transport leaves Prague for Lodz ghetto.
October 19	Terezin becomes Jewish ghetto. (Population in 1930 was 7,181; half were military men living in 11 barracks.)
1942 *from January* *to October*	Transports begin to leave for the East. Each contains about 1,000 people, among them children. (1 per cent will return.)
August 31	Terezin population: 41,552 prisoners. Space for each prisoner: 5¼ sq. ft. Average work week: 80 to 100 hours. Children from 14 years old are forced to work as adults. 106 to 156 persons die every day.
December 6	3,541 children are in Terezin; 2,000 in children's "homes."
1943 *December 31*	3,367 children in Terezin; 1,969 in children's "homes."
1944 *December 31*	819 children under 15 years old counted at Terezin.
1945 *May 7*	Terezin liberated by Red Army.

A Note on Sources

The most detailed account of Terezin, its history, daily life, and how it fitted into the Final Solution, is contained in the book *Terezin*, published in Prague in 1965 by the Council of Jewish Communities in the Czech lands. Other valuable books are: *Ghetto Theresienstadt* by Zdenek Lederer (London, 1963); *Terezin: Little Fortress* by Tana Kulisova (Prague, 1953); *The Terezin Requiem* by Josef Bor (New York, 1963); *Dokumente Theresienstadt* by H. G. Adler (Tubingen, 1958); and *We Survived* by Rabbi Leo Baeck (Yale, 1949).

On the general subject of the holocaust, I relied largely on Raul Hilberg's *The Destruction of the European Jews* (Chicago, 1961), and Gerald Reitlinger's *The Final Solution* (New York, 1961). Both are classics of their time and required reading for any comprehension of the Nazi era.

Finally, around a dozen survivors of Terezin in the New York area were most generous and helpful in granting me lengthy interviews. I thank Mr. Norbert Troller, the eminent architect, Mr. Fred Kantor, Mrs. Edith Ahlfeld-Schlesinger, and Mrs. Martha Klein von Peci. Understandably, some did not wish to be identified. I owe all these people my lasting gratitude and esteem.

GERALD GREEN